The Manager's Guide to
Psychological Safety

The Manager's Guide to Psychological Safety

David D. Van Fleet

BEP

BUSINESS EXPERT PRESS

Leader in applied, concise business books

The Manager's Guide to Psychological Safety

Cover design by Charlene Kronstedt

Interior design by Exeter Premedia Services Private Ltd., Chennai, India

First published in 2025 by
Business Expert Press, LLC
222 East 46th Street, New York, NY 10017
www.businessexpertpress.com

ISBN-13: 978-1-63742-818-4 (paperback)
ISBN-13: 978-1-63742-819-1 (e-book)

Business Expert Press Human Resource Management and Organizational Behavior Collection

First edition: 2025

10 9 8 7 6 5 4 3 2 1

EU SAFETY REPRESENTATIVE
Mare Nostrum Group B.V.
Mauritskade 21D
1091 GC Amsterdam
The Netherlands
gpsr@mare-nostrum.co.uk

Description

***The Manager's Guide to Psychological Safety* presents a simple and easy-to-understand way to achieve psychological safety in organizations.** Psychological safety is an organizational culture where no one will be punished for asking questions, speaking their minds, reporting mistakes and talking about them, and expressing concerns or proposing new ideas without being asked.

While relevant topics such as change, communication, motivation, and safety are covered, the concern is with the people in organizations—assuring that they are treated with dignity and respect for the benefit of all, thus creating for them a psychologically safe place in which to work.

Approaches to achieving psychological safety are presented and present a unique framework (V-REEL) for analyzing the organization and its internal environment that may hinder or help it become psychologically safe. Psychological safety, once attained, enhances the organization's reputation and its bottom line.

Contents

Testimonials

"I absolutely loved the read and enjoyed the book's flow and relevance to my work in addressing the unspoken impact of psychological trauma. It nailed it for me from the standpoint of process in pursuing desired continuous results/ objectives. The safety section and the long-term negative impact touched me in terms of end results and the inability to bring closures because of situations. The case studies offered were evidence of achievable success when leaders stuck to the plan. Shooting from the hip always seems comfortable but baseless when formed from a gut reaction. I fell in love with the approach as a relative application to my workplace security management consultant utilizing a robust, agile and proactive approach, and unique process. Finally, it was surprisingly reader-friendly, engaging the reader as I read it. It was enlightening, informative, and educationally full of actionable considerations in bringing all levels of readership to a tiered level of understanding and application and consideration. It is a leadership-focused guide that takes the reader up the next rung on the ladder of relativity, application, and beyond. This book will be the sister reference guide right along with my combating workplace violence philosophy, consulting, and training. Dr. David Van Fleet hit a home run out of my ballpark."—**Felix P. Nater, President and Owner of Nater Associates, Ltd. A human resource security management consulting practice focusing on workplace violence and security consulting.**

"I wanted to reach out to express my gratitude for your invaluable work on The Manager's Guide to Psychological Safety. *Each chapter delves so deeply into essential themes of psychological safety, communication, motivation, and leadership—all crucial elements in fostering a positive, effective workplace. Your ability to break down these topics, from the origins of psychological safety to the nuances of organizational relationships and change management, truly stands out.*

I especially appreciated how you interwove case studies and reflective questions throughout each chapter. These additions bring the theory to life, making it more engaging and applicable for readers to connect to their own experiences and challenges. The 'V-REEL' framework and the practical guidance in 'Guides to Action' have been particularly insightful, offering both strategic and actionable advice. The psychological safety models and your structured 'Think About This Chapter' prompts encourage a reflective and practical approach to these vital topics.

Thank you again for contributing such a valuable resource to the field. Your work informs and inspires meaningful change, offering readers a comprehensive toolkit to improve workplace dynamics and foster supportive environments. I look forward to applying many of the insights and models you presented and will keep this book close as a trusted resource."—**Salem M. Altuhaih, Certified Management Consultant and Professor of Management at Kuwait University**

"Utilizing his extensive grasp of managerial science, Dr. Van Fleet has created a 'go-to-resource' for managers challenged by ever-shifting business paradigms. A rare combination of research and practice, this is a book that should be on every business leader's reading list."—**Ernie Stark, Former Editor, Journal of Behavioral and Applied Management**

Preface

My goal in writing *The Manager's Guide to Psychological Safety* was to present to managers and nonmanagers a simple and easy-to-understand way to achieve psychological safety in their organizations. To do so, first, some fundamental concepts are covered—psychological safety and who managers are. Next, other necessary topics are discussed—change, communication, motivation, and safety. Then, I cover approaches to achieving psychological safety and present a unique framework (V-REEL) for analyzing the organization and its internal environment that may hinder or help it become psychologically safe.

It should be noted, though, that this book focuses on psychological safety that, if attained, could enhance an organization's reputation and possibly its bottom line and not on what behaviors are legal versus illegal. It is up to lawyers and legislators to wrestle with issues of legality. The concern here is with people in organizations—assuring that they are treated with dignity and respect for the benefit of all in order to become psychologically safe.

Acknowledgments

The philosophy underlying this work owes a debt to the work of Flint (2018) and Morrison (2017). Their concepts guided the development of the unique approach developed in this book.

Educational Features

The Manager's Guide to Psychological Safety presents six educational features: readable, interesting, up-to-date, accurate, unique, and audience. The first two ensure that the book is readily understandable by a diverse audience, while others ensure that it is of high quality and targeted to those most likely to need it.

Readable

To ensure readability, unnecessary jargon is avoided. The use of straightforward language that involves the reader and a logical sequencing of material contributes to making the material clear and understandable to you, the reader.

Interesting

The material is realistic and interesting to make learning easier and more enjoyable. A variety of "tools" are provided to make applications of the material relevant and understandable to you and your group or team.

Up-to-Date

To be on the cutting edge means to have the most up-to-date material available. I have striven to make the material current and timely.

Accurate

Numerous sources are provided. Careful use of research assures that the material is accurate, while practical examples assure that it is relevant.

Audience

The Manager's Guide to Psychological Safety is written at a level that is appropriate for individuals in either self-study, training, or classroom settings. The reader needs no special business, organizational, or technical background to understand this book. However, the more experience in organizations that the reader has, the more the reader will recognize the value of the material.

Unique

Finally, *The Manager's Guide to Psychological Safety* differs from other self-help time-management books in that it focuses on psychological safety and a unique method (V-REEL) for attaining it.

CHAPTER 1

What Is Psychological Safety?

Psychological safety is the key to creating a workplace where people can be confident enough to act without undue fear of being ridiculed, punished, or fired—and be humble enough to openly doubt what is believed and done.[*]

Origins[1]

The origins of psychological safety can be traced to 1844, when Soren Kierkegaard identified creativity as two forces that produced anxiety. In 1942, Joseph Schumpeter identified a pattern of creative destruction, where innovation destroys and creates new ways; in 1943, Abraham Maslow identified "belongingness needs," where the physiological and safety needs are fairly well gratified; and in 1947, Herbert Simon suggested that fully functioning organizations need friendliness and cooperation. In 1954, clinical psychologist Carl Roger used the term in a collection of papers on creativity. Then, in 1960, Douglas McGregor referred to nonphysical "security needs."

Finally, Edgar H. Schein and Warren G. Bennis, based on concepts originally developed at the National Training Laboratories Institute for Applied Behavioral Science, known as the NTL Institute in Bethel, Maine, coined the term in their book, *Personal and Organizational Change Through Group Methods: The Laboratory Approach*, which they defined as psychological safety is a climate, "which encourages provisional tries and which tolerates failure without retaliation, renunciation, or guilt" (Schein

---

[*] This section is adapted from www.leaderfactor.com/post/the-history-of-psychological-safety.

and Bennis 1965). The NTL Institute is now located in Silver Spring, Maryland, but continues the same work as before. Schein and Bennis noted that individuals should develop self-awareness, and as they do, both individuals and group members benefit from situations that enable integrated decisions by the group. This integration of decision making seemed to create situations that were psychologically safe for everyone in the group.

Michael (1976) explored the social psychological conditions necessary for changing the norms and structure of organizations and noted that groups perform better when they acknowledge and learn from mistakes, whether by themselves or others. Then Kahn (1990) wrote about meaningfulness, safety, and availability as conditions that shape how individuals define their roles in the group or organization. He indicated that psychological safety occurred in organizations where conditions were more or less nonthreatening and predictable and had consistent social situations in which members could engage one another. He explained that in order for employees to feel engaged at work, which is a key ingredient in effective performance. The same concepts are suggested in the further work of Schein (1993), but even more specifically in the work of Edmonds (1996). Her research suggested that psychological safety was an important management issue where the task "becomes the design and nurturance of work environments in which it is possible to learn from mistakes and collectively to avoid making the same ones in the future" (Edmonds 1996, 25). Learning as well as safety/security combine to ensure that organization members are comfortable and not threatened while doing their tasks. More recently, Google, in 2014, conducted "Project Aristotle," a study of 180 of its own teams for a period of three years. It determined that psychological safety was a defining characteristic of high-performing teams. Deming (2018) suggests eliminating fear *so that everyone may work effectively for the organization* in point 8 of his 14 Points for Management.

Definitions

The chapter started with Sutton's definition, "Psychological safety is the key to creating a workplace where people can be confident enough to act without undue fear of being ridiculed, punished, or fired—and be humble enough to openly doubt what is believed and done." Another definition specific to teams is, "Team psychological safety is a shared belief held by members of a team that it's OK to take risks, to express their ideas and concerns, to speak up with questions, and to admit mistakes—all without fear of negative consequences" (Gallo 2023). Psychological safety has also been defined as "an interpersonal climate in which individuals feel able to take interpersonal risks without fear of negative consequences" (https://psychsafety.co.uk/about-psychological-safety/).

Other definitions vary, but they share much in common such as "The term refers to a group trait: A climate in which people feel free and safe to ask questions, dare to speak their minds, are empowered to address and refute one another, where they report mistakes and talk about them, and express concerns or propose new ideas without being asked" (Van der Loo and Beks 2020, 14). Another view is that psychological safety is "a belief that one will not be punished or humiliated for speaking up with ideas, questions, concerns, or mistakes" (Helbig and Norman 2023, 2). This same view seems to be shared by Radecki and Ancona (2021, 22).

Nevertheless, psychological safety is most frequently defined essentially, as Edmonds proposed. She offered this definition: "Psychological safety is created by leaders who have the humility and courage to seek ideas and insights from the employees they serve. This is how to create a learning culture and encourage followers to become their best" (https://amycedmondson.com/psychological-safety/). Thus, psychological safety is frequently described as a shared belief among individuals regarding whether it is safe to engage in interpersonal risk-taking in the workplace (Newman, Donohue, and Eva 2017). With regard to teams, it is defined as "a shared belief held by members of a team that it's OK to take risks, to express their ideas and concerns, to speak up with questions, and to admit mistakes—all without fear of negative consequences" (Gallo 2023).

The crucial point in all of these various definitions is that psychological safety involves managerial or organizational actions that help people feel purposeful, motivated, and energized to achieve their best performance at work (Cable 2018). Cable also suggests that the best way to achieve this is by adopting the humble mindset of a servant leader who envisions their key role as serving or helping other organization members as they explore and grow while providing tangible and emotional support as they do so. Servant leaders display a style that is based on the idea that leaders prioritize serving the greater good. Leaders with this style serve their team and organization first. They don't prioritize their own objectives. Servant leaders create a culture of learning and an atmosphere that encourages followers to become the very best of which they are capable.

How Psychological Safety Relates to Performance Standards

Edmonson (1999), using the concept of team psychological safety, defined as a shared belief that the team is safe for interpersonal risk-taking, developed the following model (Figure 1.1) to indicate the notion of team learning, which is seen as a shared belief held by members of a team that the team is safe for interpersonal risk-taking. That shared belief, coupled with efficacy and team learning behavior, leads to a performance that satisfies customer needs and expectations.

While psychological safety has predominantly been associated with teams or small groups, there is no reason it cannot apply to whole organizations, especially if the underlying conditions are understood.

Delizonna (2017, 5) states that psychological safety leads to "higher levels of engagement, increased motivation to tackle difficulty problems, more learning and development opportunities, and better performance." Sameer (2023) suggests that psychological safety can improve organizational performance in at least four ways. It promotes innovation

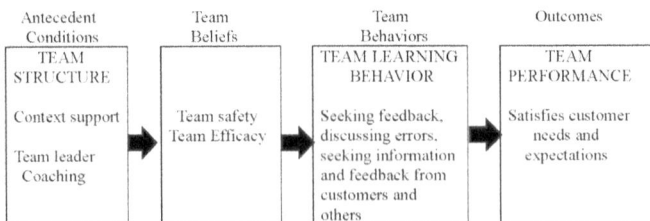

Antecedent Conditions	Team Beliefs	Team Behaviors	Outcomes
TEAM STRUCTURE Context support Team leader Coaching	Team safety Team Efficacy	TEAM LEARNING BEHAVIOR Seeking feedback, discussing errors, seeking information and feedback from customers and others	TEAM PERFORMANCE Satisfies customer needs and expectations

Source: Adapted from Edmondson, A. C. (1999). Psychological Safety and Learning Behavior in Work Teams. Administrative Science Quarterly, 44(2), p. 357.

Figure 1.1 Edmonson's model of work-team learning

Source: Adapted from Edmondson, A.C. 1999. Psychological Safety and Learning Behavior in Work Teams, Administrative Science Quarterly 44(2): 357.

and creativity since when individuals feel psychologically safe, they will be more likely to share their ideas and take risks. It also enhances employee engagement by creating a sense of belonging and purpose. Psychological safety can improve communication and collaboration since individuals feel more comfortable expressing their thoughts and opinions. Finally, it reduces turnover and absenteeism because individuals will likely be satisfied with their jobs. Kim, Lee, and Connerton (2020) echo these and found that psychological safety is the engine of performance, contributing to group performance and enhancing group processes.

Conditions

As shown in Figure 1.2, three underlying conditions must be met to achieve psychological safety. There need be no order to these conditions as any one or two could be accomplished without the others. However, understanding is clearly involved. Members of the organization must know the "why" for doing something, why a particular activity should take place, or even if it should take place. "If I don't understand what's going on, why should I get involved?" is a sentiment indicating that the individual needs to be educated in the why and how of the organization and particular activities involved.

Figure 1.2 Underpinnings of psychological safety

Understanding involves not just little things but also the big picture. Organizational members should also care about the organization and the particular activity. They should want to see the activity take place, and they should want to see the organization succeeding, too. "I care about seeing things get done, but it's not my job" is another sentiment that might be heard. Helping the individual to understand more fully what and why something needs to be done could lessen this response.

Organizational members should also accept their roles and responsibilities in carrying out the organization's activities. Organizational members may be careless and lackadaisical since "It really doesn't matter because someone else will fix any problems that occur." Once again, it is important to educate the individual about what and why something needs to be done and their role in the organization.

Any combination of two conditions—understanding, caring, and/or acceptance—would lead to less-than-optimal results for the individual and the organization. Indeed, any two together could simply lead to frustration on the part of the individual, which in turn could cause them to quit or do even less.

Impediments

Unfortunately, there are many impediments or obstacles to achieving psychological safety. Passive aggressive managers are a major impediment (the following is based on MacArthur, 2023). They make commitments but don't intend to keep them. They punish members for errors but never praise them for doing things right. They may tell you how to do something, but then change the way they want it done. Or they may simply ignore others, providing no real leadership. Managers who use domination to get things done can also be impediments. These managers rarely, if ever, involve group members in the decision. Members learn to rely on the manager to make decisions and solve problems even though they are capable of doing things themselves. This lack of inclusion is particularly damaging to underrepresented members of the organization. Finally, low or no risk tolerance can lead managers to try to do everything by themselves.

Safe Work Australia has compiled an extensive list of psychosocial hazards to psychological safety (www.safeworkaustralia.gov.au/safety-topic/managing-health-and-safety/mental-health/psychosocial-hazards). In addition to impeding psychological safety and, hence, emotional injury, some of them can also cause physical harm or injury. That list is as follows:

- Bullying
- Conflict
- Poor workplace relationships and interactions
- Harassment, including sexual and gender-based harassment
- Inadequate rewards and recognition
- Lack of role clarity
- Low job control
- Poor organizational change management
- Poor organizational justice
- Poor physical environment
- Poor support
- Remote or isolated work
- Too many job demands
- Traumatic events or material
- Violence and aggression

In addition, Jiang et al. (2019) have shown that hiding can also be a barrier to psychological safety.

With such impediments as these, it is hard to believe that psychological safety could ever be achieved, but it has been achieved, and perhaps by using the information in this book, it will be achieved in your organization.

Before taking steps to achieve psychological safety, several concepts need to be explored and their connection to psychological safety identified and clarified. Those concepts include exactly who a manager is, what changes in the organization or personnel may be involved to achieve psychological safety, how communication will occur and what form that communication will take, what is the motivation for the necessary changes, and finally, what roles do environmental and physical safety have in psychological safety. After establishing this background, a unique framework (V-REEL) will be introduced as a powerful method for achieving psychological safety. Finally, specific guidelines for behavior or action are presented. In this way, this book should be used to educate everyone in an organization as to what constitutes psychological safety and, more importantly, what can be done now to try to achieve it.

Case Study

I work in a manufacturing firm; however, my job is planning and not actually doing the operations. While I handle all routine plans and projects, Matt is supposed to do projects that come in after a certain time (late in the month). Frequently, he will come to me and say that he doesn't know how to do a project, although he has done similar ones before. I always show him what to do, but that means that I actually end up doing it. I'm tired of this, but if I refuse, he complains to the coordinator and says that I'm being uncooperative.

I met with the coordinator, but her view was, "This sounds like something the two of you need to work out among yourselves." While this was not a totally unexpected response, it did nothing to make me feel better about the situation. I am fearful that, if this continues, I may do something drastic to Matt or the coordinator. Or maybe I should just quit.

Case Questions

1. Is this a psychologically safe workplace? Why or why not?
2. What action do you feel the writer will take? Be specific, and be sure to indicate why the action would be taken.
3. What do you think of the coordinator's response? How would you have responded or handled this if you were the coordinator?
4. What changes might you suggest for this organization?

Think About This Chapter

Take a few minutes to prepare responses to these questions and actions. In particular, managers should do this to be better prepared to achieve psychological safety in their organizations.

Chapter Questions

1. Where would your organization be located on Edmondson's chart? Try to be specific in locating your organization.
2. How can your organization move to a better location on Edmondson's Chart? Be as specific as you can.
3. Which of the underpinnings needs the most attention in your organization? How might you assist in bringing about more attention?
4. What actions have you or your organization taken to try to achieve psychological safety? Again, be specific.

Actions

Draft a policy statement regarding psychological safety that is specific to your organization.

CHAPTER 2

Psychological Contracts and Managers

Since the foremen realize the employees in this system will tend to produce optimally under passive leadership, and since the employees agree, a relationship may be hypothesized to evolve between the employees and the foremen which might be called the "psychological work contract." The employee will maintain the high production, low grievances, and so on, if the foremen guarantee and respect the norms of the employee informal culture (i.e., let the employees alone, make certain they make adequate wages, and have secure jobs).

—Argyris (1960)

A psychological contract refers to the expectations held by a member of an organization about what he or she will contribute to the organization and what the organization will provide in return. The individual contributes to the organization through effort, skills, ability, time, and loyalty. In return, the organization provides inducements to the members. Some inducements, like pay or benefits, are tangible, while others, like status or prestige, are intangible. When individuals join an organization because they think they can make an impact, earn attractive salaries, or have opportunities to advance, then those organizational members will expect those to occur. As shown in Figure 2.1, those relations can lead to violent or nonviolent behavior on the part of those in the organization.

Jay (n.d.) indicates that there are four types of psychological contracts: transactional, transitional, balanced, and relational. Transactional refers to the relationship between an employee and an organization, emphasizing

	Low	High
High	Moderate likelihood of violent behavior	Highest likelihood of violent behavior
Individual Predispositions for Violent Behavior	Some likelihood of non-violent behavior	Moderate likelihood of non-violent or violent behavior
Low	Lowest likelihood of violent behavior	Some likelihood of non-violent aggressive or retaliatory behavior

Organizational Propensity to Elicit
Dysfunctional Behavior

Figure 2.1 Individual and organizational relations to violent/ dysfunctional behavior

the exchange of specific tasks and rewards. Transitional occurs during organizational changes or transitions, such as mergers, acquisitions, or restructuring. It reflects the expectations and obligations that employees have during periods of change. Balanced contracts emphasize fair and equitable exchanges between employees and organizations. Relational ones focus on building long-term relationships between employees and organizations.

If both the member and the organization perceive that the psychological contract is fair and equitable, they will be satisfied with the relationship and will continue to follow it. However, a change may occur if either party sees an imbalance or inequity. For example, the member may ask for a different assignment or a change in compensation. The member may decrease the effort he or she puts forward or look for a better fit with another organization. The organization can also initiate change by reassigning the member to another position, asking them to improve their skills through training, or, as a last resort, even terminating the individual's membership altogether.

A challenge faced by any organization, then, is to manage these psychological contracts. An organization must ensure that it is getting value from its employees and that they are achieving the goals set for them by the organization. At the same time, the organization must also be sure that it provides employees with appropriate inducements and a work environment free from threats.

Organizational Relationships

The nature of organizational relationships is as varied as the organization's individual members. Personality, past experiences, and attitudes, as well as numerous other factors, affect those relationships. You need to strive for organizational relationships that are personal and positive. You are likely to achieve this when the individual members of the organization know each other, share mutual respect and friendship, enjoy interacting with one another, and enjoy or at least don't resent the organization. In most organizational relationships, members interact professionally, focused on goal accomplishment. These relationships, whether positive or negative, exist among individuals, among groups, and among individuals and groups, but they can also change over time.

Effective working relationships promote collaboration and cooperation—people working together toward the organization's best interests while also achieving their own personal goals. Good working relationships in a psychologically safe environment are a tremendous source of synergy, where that refers to the interaction or cooperation of two or more individuals to produce a combined effect greater than the sum of their separate effects. With psychological safety, people support one another, work well together, and accomplish much more than those that do not. The focus is on meeting goals and accomplishing tasks; they are more inclined to help each other. And even when people are working individually, the presence of good relations minimizes emotional distractions.

The psychological contract that underlies psychological safety can be very strong, but note that it is not necessarily long-lasting. You have to keep focused on organizational relationships in order to keep it in place.

Why Managers?

Why managers and why you? Before thinking about "why managers," consider first just what it is that managers do and who, then, is a manager.

What and Who

A textbook definition of managers in organizations is that they are those individuals in a group or organization who engage in activities directed at the efficient and effective utilization of resources in the pursuit of one or more goals (Griffin 2022; DuBrin 2009: Gomez-Mejia, Balkin, and Cardy 2008; Van Fleet and Peterson 1994).

Expanding on that definition, it should be obvious that organizational managers are active. Organizational managers do not sit around all day and think. Even if they sit in one place behind a desk, they talk, listen, read, write, meet, observe, and participate. Most of these managerial activities can involve planning to get something done; organizing resources to get it done; leading, directing, guiding, or helping to get it done; staffing, ensuring the availability of people to accomplish what needs to be done, or controlling the important elements necessary to get it done.

While organizational managers use a variety of resources to get things done, they try to use those resources efficiently (without wasting time, effort, or resources) and effectively (they are successful, they accomplish things, and get it done). The resources may be human resources (people—volunteers, assembly-line workers, managers, and dealers for a car manufacturer like Honda), physical resources (things—office supplies, buildings, furniture, and raw materials for a chemical company like DuPont), financial resources (money—donations, retained earnings, product sales, and bank loans for a retail company like Walmart), or informational resources (data—charities helped, sales projections and market research for a company like Procter & Gamble).

The definition also indicates the importance of a goal or goals. Goals are the objectives, aims, or targets the group or organization strives to achieve. Organizational managers must set or participate in setting goals that are appropriate for their group or organization. Goals can be developed for many different areas and levels within a large organization and can change over time. Goals may be simple and easy for anyone to see or complex and vague and difficult for many people to understand. They may be capable of being achieved in a short time, or they may take years to achieve fully.

Complex

Organizational management is a complex process. Partly because of the different activities they engage in but also because what organizational managers do changes frequently. Organizational managers get interrupted every nine minutes (https://managementblog.org/2005/08/16/whats-your-discipline/), as they typically are engaged in more than one activity at a time. Juggling multiple activities can serve as a source of excitement and a reward for those seeking new challenges, but it can also be tiring and dysfunctional. It always requires enormous energy.

A recent study found that organizational managers spend most of their time on "paperwork" (Ryba 2021). Specifically, it found that managers spend:

- 54 percent of their time on administrative (paper) work;
- 30 percent on solving problems and collaborating with other managers;
- 10 percent on strategy and innovation; and
- 7 percent on developing people and engaging with stakeholders (e.g., investors, employees, customers, and suppliers).

	URGENT	NOT URGENT
IMPORTANT	**DO** Tasks that need immediate attention and have high importance. Emergency medical issue or project due tomorrow.	**PLAN** Long-term tasks that are crucial but not time-sensitive. These are often bigger goals, like plan expansion.
	DELEGATE	**ELIMINATE**
NOT IMPORTANT	Attending noncritical meetings or finishing menial paperwork.	Tasks that would be nice to get to but aren't a priority, such as rearrange the office layouts.

Figure 2.2 Eisenhower Matrix

Managers to be effective should use the Eisenhower Matrix as indicated in Figure 2.2 (www.perfony.com/en/history-of-the-eisenhower-matrix/). Attributed to General Dwight D. Eisenhower, the Matrix focuses a manager's attention on those things that really matter while delegating, planning, or eliminating other elements of the work (www.inc.com/nick-hobson/69-years-ago-president-eisenhower-came-up-with-best-matrix-for-making-better-decisions.html).

Quadrant 1—Important and urgent. Tasks in this category require immediate attention and are crucial to achieving goals and meeting deadlines. Effective leaders prioritize tasks in this quadrant to address critical issues promptly. By tackling these tasks head-on, leaders can prevent potential crises and maintain a proactive approach to their responsibilities.

Quadrant 2—Important but not urgent. Tasks that are significant but do not have an immediate deadline or require immediate attention are here. Effective leaders allocate sufficient time for these important but not urgent tasks. They may involve long-term planning, goal setting, skill development, and relationship building.

Quadrant 3—Urgent but not important. These tasks are often distractions or interruptions that hinder productivity. Effective leaders aim to minimize time spent on these or delegate them whenever possible. Leaders can improve their efficiency and maintain focus on strategic objectives by reducing the time spent on tasks that do not contribute directly to goals.

Quadrant 4—Not urgent and not important. These tasks that are not urgent nor important. They are time-wasters and can include excessive social media use, unproductive meetings, or trivial activities that make leaders fall prey to "action addiction." Effective leaders minimize or eliminate these tasks to free up time for more meaningful and productive activities.

Organizational managers are not directly focusing on those in their group or the goals that they should be pursuing. Correcting that is a goal for this book.

Pervasiveness

Another characteristic of managerial work in organizations is its pervasiveness—its influence and applicability in many different situations. For example, some of the organizations that you might come into contact with might be the Coca-Cola that you buy from Safeway that was sold to the store by a local distributor, who bought it from a licensed bottler, who in turn purchased the syrup from the Coca-Cola Company.

Organizational management is not something that exists only in businesses. It can be found in universities, government agencies, health care organizations, social organizations, and families. Indeed, organizational management and organizational managers are in every collection of people who find it necessary to coordinate their activities to accomplish something.

Levels

If we take a hypothetical organization and draw two horizontal lines through it, we commonly classify organizational managers as top, middle, and first line. The dividing lines are arbitrary, but top management refers to those at the upper levels of the organization and usually includes the chief executive officer (CEO) and vice presidents of the organization. Top organizational managers set overall organizational goals, determine strategy and operating policies, and represent the organization to the external environment. In business and nonbusiness organizations, top organizational managers may be called CEO, chief operating officer (COO), executive director, or director of a specific area. The titles used vary considerably from those mentioned here and may be unique to a particular organization.

Middle organizational managers extend from top management down to those immediately above first-line management. In business organizations, they include such titles and positions as plant manager, division manager, and operations manager. In nonbusiness organizations, they may be called coordinators, administrators, or specialists. Although the middle manager's job is changing, and some experts warn that the future of such positions is questionable, these managers generally implement the strategies and policies set by top managers and coordinate the work of lower-level managers.

First-line managers are those who supervise operating employees. In businesses, they are called by titles such as supervisor, department manager, office manager, and foreman. In nonbusiness organizations, the titles may be supervisors, leaders, counselors, or advisers. In contrast to middle and top managers, these first-line managers spend much of their time directly overseeing or looking after the work of operating or "rank and file" employees or members of the organization.

Areas

Another useful way of differentiating among kinds of organizational managers is by their area of concern. Common areas are marketing, operations, finance, and human resources. Marketing managers develop policies for pricing, promoting, and distributing the products and services of the firm. Operations managers oversee the creation of the organization's goods and services. Finance managers handle the financial assets of the organization. They oversee accounting systems, manage investments, control disbursements, and maintain and provide the top managers with relevant information about the firm's financial health. Another important area of management is human resources management (HRM). Human resource managers determine future human resource needs, oversee recruiting and hiring the right kind of people to fill those needs, design effective compensation and performance appraisal systems, and ensure that various legal guidelines and regulations are followed. Other kinds of managers include public relations, research and development, international, and administrative or general managers who are generalists, overseeing a variety of activities in many different areas.

So?

So, why organizational managers? Because they are in positions to have an impact, to change the organization's culture, to bring about psychological safety. However, even if you are not an organizational manager, you are a manager. You manage yourself; you manage your behavior, dress, opinions, thought processes, and everything about you. And, in doing so, you influence those around you. Thus, this book is written for you, a manager, yourself, or for an organization. This book is intended to assist you in transforming your group, club, team, or organization into a psychologically safe one. In order to do so, you must communicate with others.

Several approaches to obtaining psychological safety have been proposed, but there seems to be some common ground. Communication is important and must be open and inclusive (Helbig and Norman 2023; Van der Loos and Beks 2020). It cannot just be the leader or manager outlining a process but must involve sharing—the active participation of all parties (Van der Loos and Beks 2020). Errors and mistakes must be acknowledged and reframed as learning opportunities (Edmonson 2019; Wegner n.d.). But someone has to take the initiative; someone has to get the ball rolling. That someone is you, the manager.

You, as the manager, set the stage for change to occur by building trust through transparency in communication (Wegner n.d.), including being accessible or approachable, admitting mistakes, framing the work, emphasizing participation, demonstrating humility, expressing appreciation, and setting boundaries (Edmonson 2012, 139 and 2019). You must also hold your tongue and be careful in what you say. These concepts have been referred to as the four pillars of effective teaming—Speaking up, Collaboration, Experimentation, and Reflection (Edmonson 2012).

Even if you are NOT an organizational manager, the ideas in this book will enable you to assist those who are organizational managers in your organization. You will need to communicate with them and help them understand the importance of psychological safety.

Case Study

I own a small restoration business. I, along with my six regular workers and any necessary temporary workers, repair, restore, paint, and generally fix older properties so that they are nearly as good as new. I work hard with all of my workers in order to have good relations and to keep costs as low as we can without causing anyone to be uncomfortable or to quit. Keeping costs low is important for me in order to bid competitively on jobs. However, I've got a competitor who calls and threatens me whenever we are bidding on the same job. He is a bully and just might carry out his threats, so I have backed out of bidding any time that we are trying to get the same job. Several of my regular workers have told me that I should bid against him anyway and that if he carries out his threats, he will have to answer to the law. I'm thinking about it as I respect my workers.

Case Questions

1. In what way is this restoring company a psychologically safe workplace? Why or why not? Be specific.
2. If the business is not psychologically safe, how might the owner behave to make it more so? Again, be specific in your response.
3. Should the owner listen to his regular workers and submit bids in competition with the bully competitor? Why or why not?
4. Would competing help or hinder this organization in its efforts to be more psychologically safe?

Think About This Chapter

Take a few minutes to prepare responses to these questions and actions. In particular, managers should do this to be better prepared to achieve psychological safety in their organizations.

Chapter Questions

1. Where would you locate yourself on the chart in Figure 2.1? That is, what is your individual predisposition for violence? Try to be specific in locating yourself.
2. How can you move to a better position on that chart? That is, what can you do so that your individual predisposition for violence is reduced?
3. What actions could your organization take to help you reduce your individual predisposition for violence and move to a better position on that chart?
4. Would the Eisenhower Matrix assist you in moving the organization in the direction of being psychologically safe?

Actions

Look at the draft policy statement regarding psychological safety that you made in the first chapter. How would you change it now?

CHAPTER 3

Change

The only way that we can live is if we grow. The only way that we can grow is if we change. The only way that we can change is if we learn. The only way we can learn is if we are exposed. And the only way that we can become exposed is if we throw ourselves out into the open.
Do it. Throw yourself.

— C. JoyBell C

Learning and change will be necessary to bring about psychological safety in your organization. You may need to change, and, of course, your organization will need to change. Before attempting this change or any other major effort to alter your organization's culture, it would be useful to understand how the change process occurs in organizations. Managing that change, or any change for that matter should be made rationally and logically to ensure that the change will be successful.

First, consider why the change is necessary. There may be sociocultural pressures and even political–legal pressures causing you to introduce psychological safety to your organization, or you may wish to do so for personal reasons. In any event, psychological safety should apply to your organization's members, suppliers, customers, and any and all those with whom the organization interacts. Generally, bringing about change involves a sequence or series of steps along the way.

Steps in Change

A widely used framework indicating steps to be followed in achieving change is that of Kotter (Kotter 1996). Kotter's framework consists of eight steps as follows:

Create a Sense of Urgency. Inspire people to act—with passion and purpose—to achieve a bold, aspirational opportunity.

Build a Guiding Coalition. Have a committee or group to guide the change effort.

Form a Strategic Vision. Creating interactive and engaging goals.

Enlist a Volunteer Army. Expand the coalition to broaden its impact.

Enable Action. Remove barriers to change.

Generate Short-Term Wins. Use short-term victories to inspire continued change efforts.

Sustain Acceleration. Keep the momentum going.

Institute Change. Finalize and incorporate the change throughout the organization.

More generally, the first step is the recognition of a need for change. After determining that a change is needed to achieve psychological safety, goals should be established for the change. Consider why the change is necessary, what should be gained by making the change, and how the change will be implemented. The third step involves diagnosis. This means that you should look carefully at the organizational system to identify all the possible effects of the change, both good and bad. Try to see the change from the points of view of others and note which parts are likely to be readily accepted and which are likely to encounter resistance and from whom.

At this point, you would determine the manner in which the change would take place. Will it involve changes in policies, personnel, procedures, equipment, or some combination of these or all of them? The dynamics associated with the change must also be carefully planned. Will training be done, who will do it, and who will be trained? Will any necessary training be done "in-house," or will an outside agency be required? When these and a myriad of other questions have been answered, implementation can take place. Finally, after the change is complete, it needs to be evaluated to ensure that it has met its original goals. Assuming that the goals have been reasonably met, the process is essentially complete, although fine-tuning and constant vigilance may be in order.

Another approach to change has been suggested by Kelly in 2020. She notes (https://online.hbs.edu/blog/post/change-management-process) that "Approximately 50 percent of all organizational change initiatives are unsuccessful, highlighting why knowing how to plan for, coordinate, and carry out change is a valuable skill for managers and business leaders alike." She suggests a five-step process as follows:

Step 1—Prepare the Organization for Change.
Step 2—Craft a Vision and Plan for Change.
Step 3—Implement the Change.
Step 4—Embed Changes Within Company Culture and Practices.
Step 5—Review Progress and Analyze Results.

She then suggests that you carefully examine the process by asking a series of questions. Do you understand the forces making change necessary? Do you have a plan? How will you communicate? Have you identified potential roadblocks?

There are also other important aspects related to changes in organizations. Two that are especially critical are recognizing that people may resist change and understanding ways to overcome this resistance. You should consider each of these in more detail as part of assuring that any change effort will be successful.

Resistance to Change

Employees can be openly resistant or do so in less obvious ways. Their resistance can range from public expressions to resisting change through small behaviors or language. People in organizations resist change for a variety of reasons. Although there are a great many reasons why individuals resist change, the most common reasons for resisting change are uncertainty about the results of the change, protecting individual self-interests, differing perceptions about the change, and loss of power, status, or a feeling of comfort in the organization.

Creasey (2024) found that mid-level managers and front-line employees are the most resistant to change. He suggests that there are five reasons for that resistance:

1. Lack of awareness about the reason for the change;
2. Changes in job roles;
3. A fear of the unknown;
4. Perceived lack of support from or trust in leaders;
5. Having been excluded from change-related decisions.

Change breeds uncertainty. Some people maybe unsure if they can meet new job demands, or they may be unsure whether their job will be eliminated altogether. Many changes involve alterations in work assignments and work schedules, and thus, informal groups and close working relationships among peers are broken up or made more difficult to continue. Individuals may also feel anxious and nervous and resist the change to cope better with these feelings.

Individuals may also resist change because it threatens their own self-interests. They may feel that their status will be negatively impacted. They may feel that a loss of power, status, security, or familiarity with existing procedures will be required. This, then, can also lead to resistance.

Different perceptions also cause resistance to change. Some may feel that the change is not really necessary or that the particular changes are wrong. They may feel that the changes should be in the way the organization functions, while others think the changes should be in the rules and procedures used by the organization. Others may feel that the changes should be to operations or equipment and not impact personnel.

Finally, an individual might resist change because it leads to feelings of loss or potential disruption of informal groups and working relationships. The usual "coffee" group will be no longer possible, or those with whom you normally interact will be changed. They may feel that as a result of the changes, the organization is no longer a good place to work.

Similar to these, Thevenin-Lemoine (2023) has suggested that there are 12 fundamental or basic reasons why members of organizations will resist change. They are as follows:

1. Misunderstanding the meaning of the change;
2. Fearing the unknown;
3. Lacking skills necessary after the change;
4. Impacting the individual's personal relationship with the old ways of doing things;
5. Lacking confidence to deal with the change;
6. Believing the change is simply a passing fad;
7. Lacking consultation prior to the change;
8. Poor communication;
9. Breaking the routine;
10. Feeling that the change is too much—saturation with changes;
11. Changing the status quo;
12. Lacking a reward, remuneration, or some sort of compensation for responding positively to the change.

Abbas, on the other hand, suggests that there are eight types of resistance to change (https://changemanagementinsight.com/08_types_of_resistance_to_change/):

- Organizational resistance—when organizational factors cause resistance to change.
- Group-level resistance—when employees are gathered to challenge change.
- Individual-level resistance—when powerful individuals are against change.
- Active resistance—when employees are active in opposing change.
- Passive resistance—when employees have negative emotions about change.

- Aggressive resistance—if resistance against becomes violent.
- Covert resistance—no one is openly resistant, but they are still resistant.
- Overt resistance—when employees openly resist change.

Overcoming Resistance to Change

Burkus (2023) suggests that overcoming resistance to change can be facilitated by addressing the emotions behind it and having leaders answer four questions:

1. Do we know where we are going?
2. Do we know why we are going there?
3. Do we know we can get there?
4. Do we know that there is better than here?

Providing answers to these questions in open and honest communication would greatly enhance efforts to overcome resistance to change. This would be yet another step toward achieving psychological safety.

But to overcome resistance to change, it is important to recognize the type of resistance involved, as overcoming that resistance may be relatively easy or difficult, depending on the type. Fortunately, you can at least partially overcome resistance to change in several ways. If uncertainty is causing resistance, use participation. If members' self-interests feel threatened, communication with those members should ease the change. If members have differing perceptions regarding the change or the potential results of the change, gradually implementing the change may be helpful. If, on the other hand, members are resisting because of feelings of loss, you should carefully examine each part of the change and strive to increase the positive effects and decrease the negative ones.

Encourage participation among those involved in the change. When people participate, they feel less threatened, recognize that they have a say in what happens, and are less concerned about feelings of loss. This will then lower their resistance to the change. Allow individuals to speak up, speak their minds, and weigh in with suggestions, opinions, and concerns. But some mistakenly believe that to be heard is to be heeded when, in fact, not all suggestions will be implemented (leaderfactor.com).

Open communication (see the next chapter) also helps overcome resistance. Complete and accurate information helps remove the uncertainty that so often accompanies change, as we have noted. You should provide information relevant to the change as often as possible. Disseminate information as it becomes available and be open and receptive to questions and inquiries from others about the impending change.

Facilitation can also reduce resistance. Introducing change gradually helps minimize its impact. Being sensitive to people's concerns and helping them resolve those can also help reduce resistance. Identify the pluses and minuses associated with the change and focus on increasing the pluses while reducing the minuses.

Training can also facilitate the change. In particular, training is paramount when the change is focused more on attitudes, perceptions, behaviors, and expectations, as is changing to a psychologically safe environment. People want to grow and develop, and they are capable of making useful contributions to the organization. A later chapter will indicate what training should be involved to bring about psychological safety to your organization.

Areas of Change

Achieving psychological safety may impact several different areas of the organization. Technology, structure, and people will all be affected. The various technologies employed by the organization may be impacted. Work processes and work sequences may need to be modified. The organization's information processing could also be impacted. Who reports to whom and how performance is controlled may well be altered, and the manner in which rewards (reinforcements) are allocated will certainly change. Finally, the behavior, attitudes, expectations, and perceptions of those in the organization will change.

The impact of change on each of these areas will vary both in terms of when it will be felt and how strongly it will be felt. So, you will need to frame the situation, implement the changes gradually to make it psychologically safe to learn, recognize that you can learn from failure, be mindful of occupational and cultural boundaries, and be vigilant in monitoring the effects of your changes (Edmondson 2012, 110).

One set of suggestions involves four steps (leaderfactor.com). First, inclusion safety—you should make it clear that all ideas are worth expressing. Second, learner safety—note that criticizing something does not mean that the individual is not loyal to the organization. Third, contributor safety—separate status from opinion to ensure that all views are given equal weight. Finally, challenger safety—make it clear that all suggestions will not be implemented but should be aired and evaluated anyway.

Another way of thinking about organizational change is that it is a planned effort to infuse new energy, vitality, and strength into an organization. The general cycle that change can follow is shown in Figure 3.1. First, the organization is what might be called normal "momentum"—it is growing and effectively reaching its goals. However, at some point, the organization begins to fail in its efforts to attain its objectives. At this stage, the organization reaches a plateau and ceases to grow, or it actually begins to decline, and it is at this stage that Kotter's first step comes into play—a sense of urgency is felt by those in the organization. Then, following Kotter's steps, the change process takes place.

When the organization plateaus or declines, it's time for a change, and a period of contraction occurs. During this stage, the organization reanalyzes and begins the process of change. Next comes consolidation. During consolidation, the organization adapts to the changed conditions. Eventually, if things go well, the organization will be able to start expanding and growing once again as the change is implemented and incorporated by the organization and its members.

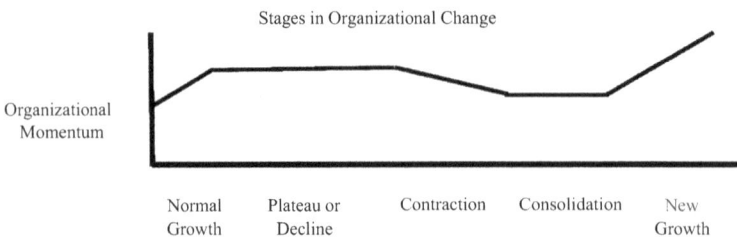

Figure 3.1 Steps in change

Change is a learning process, but remember that learning never ends. Learning is an interactive process that involves memory, attention, language, organization, processing, and even writing. It is a dynamic process that involves diagnosing or assessing the situation, designing or developing specific plans for action, treating experience as an experiment and reflection, or evaluating results (Edmondson 2012, 240–1).

Case Study

> I work for a large corporation that operates in the United States as well as in several other countries. Shortly after I was hired and began work, I was taught by senior employees that those who are tattletales won't be liked in this company, so now I don't want to report what's going on when something is not right. I would be embarrassed to admit that I couldn't somehow handle the situation, so I just put up with it and try to do the best I can. Besides, reporting it to upper management could lead to retaliation from my supervisor or another manager and just make things worse.
>
> Recently, I tried casually to bring this up to my supervisor, but if he got the message, he ignored it. Actually, I'm thankful that, if he got the message, he didn't reprimand me or change my work assignment to something on which I would be sure to fail.

Case Questions

1. Is this corporation psychologically safe? Why or why not? Try to be specific in your response.
2. Have you ever encountered an organization that frowned upon "speaking up" when something is obviously wrong? How did you handle it? Be specific.
3. If the corporation is not psychologically safe, what changes should it make to become less so?
4. If you were in this corporation, what changes in your behavior would you make? Again, be as specific as possible in your responses.

Think About This Chapter

Take a few minutes to prepare responses to these questions and actions. In particular, managers should do this to be better prepared to achieve psychological safety in their organizations.

Chapter Questions

1. Has your organization tried to systematically introduce change? If so, how successful was the effort?
2. Where would you locate your organization on the Chart in Figure 3.1? That is, at what stage is your organization? Try to be specific in locating your organization.
3. Why do you feel your organization is at that stage?
4. How can your organization accelerate a move toward the "new growth" position? Specifically, what actions should your organization take to move to the "new growth" position?

Actions

Develop a plan of action to help your organization move to the "new growth" position.

CHAPTER 4

Communication

If you look closely at your relationships, you will see that the effectiveness of your relationships is determined by how well you communicate. How well you communicate with others is determined, by and large, by how well you listen.

—Amir Fathizadeh, business coach

Communication is vital to bring about successful change to a psychologically safe organization. In the broadest sense, communication is the process of transmitting information from one person to another. However, the message being received might be quite different from the one that was transmitted. An individual might not understand what is being said, and there might be static that interrupts the process, and a letter can get lost in the mail. So, it is useful to differentiate between simple communication and effective communication. Simple communication is merely the transmission of information from one person to another. Effective communication, in contrast, occurs when the message received has essentially the same meaning as the message sent. Clearly, then, it is important to have the skills to communicate effectively. As shown in Figure 4.1, the organization's culture and general social conditions influence communication, but the individual's propensity is also important.

Communication should always be effective; however, as everyone knows, it sometimes (ofttimes?) is not. So, to better understand communication and how it might be made more effective, consider the many ways of discussing it—process, barriers, types, roles, directions, informal, and nonverbal.

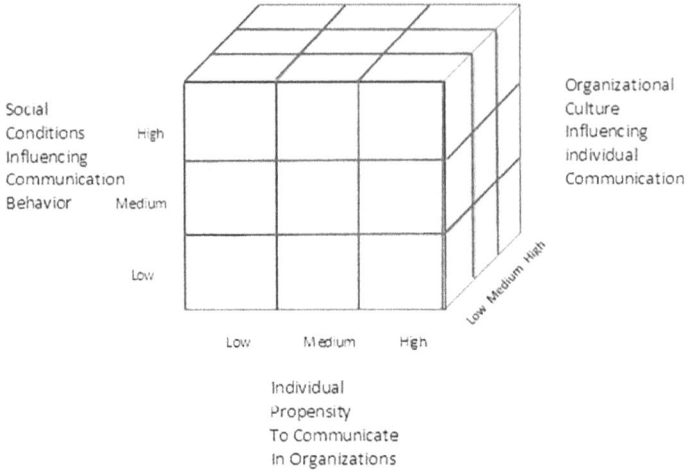

Figure 4.1 Organizational communication

Process

As shown in Figure 4.2, the message starts with the sender who encodes it (tries to put it in language understandable by the receiver). The sender then must select the channel or method by which to transmit the message (a face-to-face meeting, a letter, a telephone call, a facial expression, or any combination of these). The receiver then gets the message and decodes it.

The message is then combined with other ideas by the receiver, who may send a return message to the sender in the form of feedback, a response, or a new message. The difference between simple communication and effective communication manifests itself when the symbols are decoded into a message and combined with other ideas of the

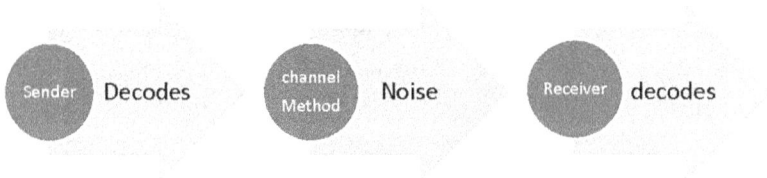

Figure 4.2 Communication process

receiver. Effective communication has occurred if the idea formed by the receiver is similar to the one originally related to the sender. On the other hand, if the ideas are different in one or more important ways, the communication is ineffective. The process may continue as two-way communication. That is, receivers may respond to the original message with a message of their own. Thus, the receiver becomes the sender, transmitting a new message to the original sender, who is now playing the role of the receiver.

Barriers

Barriers to effective communication can have a significant impact on both individual and professional lives. Communication barriers can include anything that prevents or disables communication from delivering the right message to the right person at the right time. There are three main categories of communication barriers—(1) physical communication barriers such as social distancing, remote work, deskless nature of work, closed office doors, and others; (2) emotional communication barriers resulting from emotions such as mistrust and fear; and (3) language communication barriers.

Kristina Martic in 2023 identified the top 13 communication barriers that organizations tend to encounter today (https://haiilo.com/blog/communication-barriers/). The barriers are listed here:

1. Communication skills and styles
2. Social distance and physical barriers
3. Disengagement
4. Organizational structure
5. Information overload
6. Lack of trust
7. Clarity, consistency, and frequency
8. Listening
9. Wrong communications channels
10. Demographic and cultural differences
11. Wrong communication technology

12. Lack of personalization
13. Grapevine communication

She then suggests six ways to eliminate those barriers. They are as follows:

1. Understand your multigenerational workforce;
2. Make communication more agile;
3. Create and share engaging and personalized content;
4. Switch to mobile-first communication;
5. Use the power of data and technology;
6. Leverage artificial intelligence.

She also notes that there are five working generations is many organization at present. Those generations are as follows:

- Traditionalists—born in 1945 and before
- Baby Boomers—born between 1946 and 1964
- Generation X—born between 1965 and 1976
- Millennials—born between 1977 and 1995
- Generation Z—born in 1996 and after

Understanding that each of these may require different communication styles will help to make communication more efficient.

In today's diverse workforce, language itself and cultural differences can be barriers for both senders and receivers of communications. Another barrier is noise. Noise is anything that disrupts the communication process. It can involve sound, such as someone in another room talking so loudly that two people cannot hear each other speak or a radio playing so loudly that the receiver cannot hear the sender's voice over the telephone. It can also be a letter getting lost in the mail, a telephone call being disconnected, or a typographical error in a report can all reduce communication effectiveness. Communication is also influenced by two important behavioral processes—attitudes and perception.

Attitudes are the beliefs and feelings that individuals have about specific situations, ideas, or people. Individuals have attitudes not only toward their organization and their jobs but also toward other people, politicians, sports teams, movies, and almost everything else in their lives. Attitudes impact communication in a variety of ways. If you have a positive attitude toward one individual, you will deal differently with them compared to another individual for whom you have a less positive or even negative attitude. Attitudes impact communication both from the sender and the receiver.

Perception also affects the communication process. Individuals perceiving an event may well have differing descriptions of that event. The differences are the result of differing perceptions. A major influence on perception is familiarity; that is, we tend to have perceptions based on things from which we are comfortable. One form of perception that is harmful to communication is stereotyping. Stereotyping refers to categorizing people into groups based on certain traits or qualities. We often make errors due to stereotyping the other person's ability to understand. When you see a problem as falling in a particular area, you will communicate based on that, but if you keep an open mind, you might see the problem in a different way.

Another barrier is overload. Overload occurs when the sender is transmitting so much information, or in a short period of time, that the receiver can't deal with it. So, you should monitor your communications so that you don't try to cover too much in one message. You could have other problems such as inconsistency, credibility, and reluctance. Inconsistency occurs when you send conflicting messages. Credibility problems occur when you or your information source is considered unreliable. Finally, you may be reluctant to communicate, especially if the information is bad or unpleasant. Semantic problems may involve both the sender and the receiver, especially with jargon related to a particular craft or profession. Status and power differences can also disrupt effective communication.

Receivers may have problems such as selective attention and making value judgments about the message or the sender. They may fail to pay attention by not concentrating, letting their attention wander, or looking around when the receiver is talking. Selective attention is when the receiver pays attention to only part of the message. Receivers may also make value judgments based on their beliefs about the message or the sender.

The message you intend to send may not be the message someone else receives, but when you get a message, you need to be sure that it is the one intended. You must be diligent in trying to make sure that both the sent message and the received message are the same, whether you are the sender or the receiver. Fortunately, there are things that you, as a manager, can do to overcome some or hopefully all of these problems.

As the sender in the communication process, you should be sensitive to the receiver's position. You should also solicit feedback to facilitate two-way communication. Asking the receiver if the message is understood, asking for opinions, and other such actions enhance communication effectiveness. You should also be aware of language and meaning. You should attempt to maintain credibility. There is nothing wrong with admitting that you do not know something. But you should check the facts and stay as up-to-date as possible. As a receiver, there are things that you can do. First, the receiver should be a good listener: concentrate on what is being said, look at the speaker, be patient, and pay attention. You should also attempt to be sensitive to the sender's perspective.

Types

Communication can be oral, written, or nonverbal, the latter consisting of facial expressions, body movements, and gestures to convey a message. Individuals use nonverbal communication in three ways. First, there is the setting where the communication takes place. The second is body language. Body language and pauses in speech and dress style are also parts of body language. The third aspect of nonverbal communication is the imagery conjured up by language. Nonverbal communication has advantages and disadvantages. It can provide confirming images to verbal (oral and/or written) communication, or body movements or gestures can conflict with the verbal message. When this happens, the receiver can be confused about which message to believe. Written communication, on the other hand, is generally more accurate and provides a relatively permanent record of the communication. A disadvantage is that it hinders feedback. It is also more time-consuming than oral communication. Oral communication is better when the message is personal, nonroutine, and brief. Written communication is better when the message is more imper-sonal, routine, and longer.

Roles and Direction

Your job is filled with activities that involve communication. Three roles are involved: interpersonal, decisional, and informational. Interpersonal roles involve interacting with others both within and outside the orga-nization. Decisional roles involve getting information to use in making decisions and then communicating the decisions to others. Informational roles focus specifically on acquiring and disseminating information both inside and outside the organization.

Vertical communication takes place between leaders and their fol-lowers. It can flow both down and up the organization. Downward communication helps subordinates know how the organization affects them. Upward communication is also important. It keeps managers in touch with day-to-day operations, successes and failures, and potential problems. Horizontal communication occurs between two or more col-leagues or peers at the same level in the organization. It is important for coordination and integration. The final element of organizational communication is the informal communication network that exists in all organizations.

Informal Communication

Communication invariably follows some sort of a network. A commu-nication network refers to the pattern through which group members communicate. Various patterns, such as the circle, chain, Y, and wheel, have been identified.

In the circle pattern, the sender sends the message to more than one receiver at the same time (think of a group or committee meeting). In the chain pattern, the sender sends a message to a receiver, who in turn sends it to another, and then another, and so on (clearly, there is a lot of potential for the message to become distorted). In the Y pattern, indi-viduals communicate only through a central person (the middle of the

Y). Finally, in the wheel pattern, all communication flows through one central person, who probably is the group's leader.

Another pattern is the grapevine. The grapevine is the informal communication network within an organization. It can start anywhere; some people are included in virtually all of the messages, and it flows in all directions. It exists because being social is one characteristic of human nature. People like to interact with others. Since much of this interaction involves talking, information is passed along to different people. It can be good or bad. It is quick, it builds a sense of togetherness or team spirit, and can be used to try out ideas or get informal reactions to potential decisions. On the other hand, the information along the grapevine can be inaccurate.

Yet another pattern is known as management by wandering around. In this pattern, organizational managers keep in touch with what's going on by walking around the company and talking to people. In a similar way, informal communication occurs during informal interchanges among employees that take place outside the workplace.

Nonverbal Communication

Nonverbal communication is a communication exchange that does not use words or uses words to carry more meaning than their strictest definition. Three basic types of nonverbal communication exist: images, settings, and body language. Images refer to those that are created by the kinds of words people elect to use. Settings indicate where the communication takes place. Body language refers to how we use our arms, hands, legs, and eyes, where we choose to stand, how we dress, or where we pause when speaking.

Improving Communication Effectiveness

To improve communication effectiveness, individuals can use several techniques to enhance communication effectiveness, including:

- Develop good listening skills
- Encourage two-way communication

- Be aware of language and meaning
- Maintain credibility
- Be sensitive to the receiver's perspective
- Be sensitive to the sender's perspective

Organizations can also use certain techniques to enhance communication effectiveness. These include:

- Follow up
- Regulate information flows
- Understand the richness of different media

The best advice is to communicate openly with others at all levels and respond quickly to inaccurate information. If people can come to you and get straight answers, they are less likely to pay attention to gossip and rumors. This would be a first step in developing a culture supporting psychological safety.

Case Study*

As one of the first to enter the field of office automation, Sagatec Software, Inc. had built a reputation for designing high-quality and user-friendly databases and accounting programs for business and industry. When they decided to enter the word-processing market, their engineers designed an effective, versatile, and powerful program that Sagatec felt sure would outperform any competitor.

To be sure that their new word-processing program was accurately documented, Sagatec asked the senior program designer to supervise writing the instruction manual. The result was a thorough, accurate, and precise description of every detail of the program's operation.

(Continued)

* BCcampus, Case 3. Available at: https://pressbooks.bccampus.ca/technicalwriting/chapter/casestudy-costpoorcommunication/.

When Sagatec began marketing its new word processor, cries for help flooded in from office workers who were so confused by the massive manual that they couldn't even find out how to get started. Then, several business journals reviewed the program and judged it "too complicated" and "difficult to learn." After an impressive start, sales of the new word-processing program plummeted and Sagatec went back to the drawing board.

Sagatec eventually put out a new, clearly written training guide that led new users step by step through introductory exercises and told them how to find commands quickly. But the rewrite cost Sagatec $350,000, a year's lead in the market, and it lost its reputation for producing easy-to-use business software.

Case Questions

1. Is Sagatec a psychologically safe organization? Why or why not? Be specific in your responses.
2. Consider who is communicating to whom about what, how, and why. What was the goal of the communication in each case?
3. Can you identify any communication errors at Sagatec? Like the use of inappropriate language or style? Is there poor organization or formatting of information? Can you think of other communication issues?
4. Identify possible solutions or strategies that would have prevented the problem and what benefits would be derived from implementing solutions or preventing the problem. Again, be specific.

Think About This Chapter

Take a few minutes to prepare responses to these questions and actions. In particular, managers should do this to be better prepared to achieve psychological safety in their organizations.

Chapter Questions

1. Where would you locate your organization in Figure 4.1? Try to be specific in locating your organization.
2. How can your organization accelerate a move toward a more favorable (high, high, high) position?
3. Specifically, what actions should your organization take to move to a more favorable (high, high, high) position?
4. What barriers can you identify in your organization? How might they be reduced or eliminated?

Actions

Develop a plan of action to help your organization move to a more favorable (high, high, high) position.

CHAPTER 5

Motivation

Your work is going to fill a large part of your life, and the only way to be truly satisfied is to do what you believe is great work. And the only way to do great work is to love what you do. If you haven't found it yet, keep looking. Don't settle. As with all matters of the heart, you'll know when you find it.

—Steve Jobs

Introduction

It is not enough to talk with others about psychological safety; they have to be interested in making changes. They must be motivated to make the necessary changes. Understanding human needs is a necessary starting point for understanding motivation. You need to understand why different people have different needs, why individuals' needs change, that need frustration can lead to possibly dysfunctional behavior, and how others choose to try to satisfy needs in different ways. First, the nature of motivation is examined. Then, important human needs that are relevant to the workplace are noted. Reinforcement processes are covered, and finally, a summary of how reward systems affect motivation is presented. Figure 5.1 illustrates the general framework for the motivational process.

The process starts with needs—drives or forces that initiate behavior. Individuals need recognition, feelings of accomplishment, food, affection, and the like. When needs become strong enough, they engage in efforts to fulfill them. As a result of such efforts, people experience various levels of need satisfaction. The extent to which people find their needs satisfied then influences their future efforts to satisfy the same needs. The motivational process is a dynamic one. We always have a number of needs to satisfy, and we are always at different places in the process of

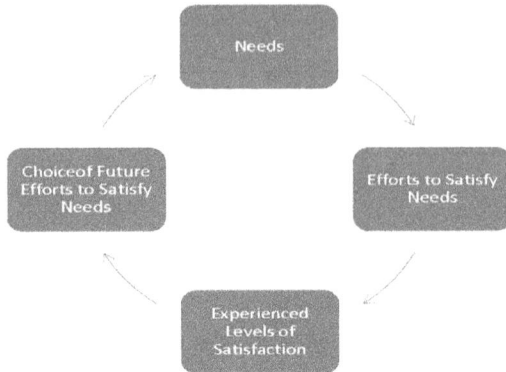

Figure 5.1 *Motivation process*

satisfying them. Likewise, different time frames are involved; satisfying hunger needs might take only a couple of hours, but satisfying the need to accomplish meaningful work can take months or years.

Three specific needs warrant mention. One of these is the need for affiliation—the need that most people have to work with others, to make friends in the workplace, and to socialize. Work settings that deprive people of social interaction may lead to dissatisfaction and low morale. Another important employee need is the need for achievement. This is the desire that some people have to excel or to accomplish some goal or task more effectively than they did in the past. Research has indicated that people with a high need for achievement tend to have four common characteristics. First, they set moderately difficult goals. Second, they want immediate feedback. Third, people with high needs to achieve tend to assume personal responsibility. Fourth, such people are often preoccupied with their tasks. Finally, the need for power is the desire to control other people and the environment. People with high power needs tend to be high performers and have good attendance records.

Another view of motivation is the expectancy model. As shown in Figure 5.2, its basic notion is simple: motivation is a function of how much we want something and how likely we think we are to get it. The problem, of course, is that in many situations, we have various outcomes—some bad and some good—to consider. The model suggests that

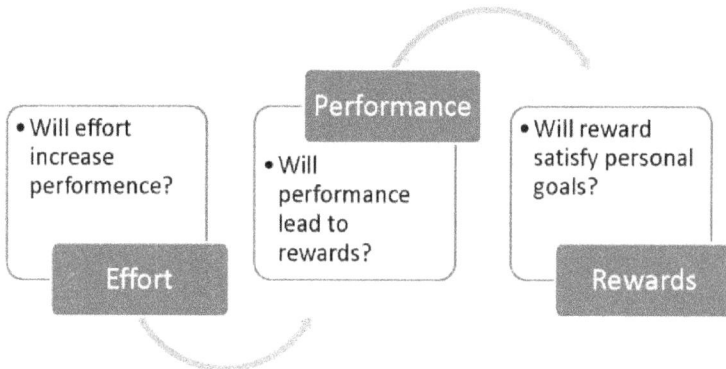

Figure 5.2 Expectancy view

motivation leads to effort, which, in conjunction with ability and environmental forces such as the availability of materials and equipment, leads to performance. Performance, in turn, has multiple outcomes. For example, high employee performance can result in several outcomes: a pay increase, a promotion, and better job assignments. However, it can also lead to stress and to the resentment of less successful colleagues. Therefore, the employee must choose how much effort to exert. Thus, it may be more accurate to argue that performance, through the reward system, leads to satisfaction rather than the reverse. This raises the notion of equity, which is also an important part of the motivation process.

With respect to psychological safety, equity is also an important consideration. Equity or fairness has been found to be a major factor influencing motivation. Given the social nature of human beings, it is no surprise that people compare their contributions and rewards to those of others. As a result of these comparisons, they may feel equity or inequity; that is, they may feel that they are treated fairly or that they are not. Equity or fairness has been found to be a major factor in determining employee motivation. First, individuals contribute to and get things from work. They contribute education, experience, expertise, time, and effort, and in return, get pay, security, recognition, and so forth. However, individuals compare contributions and rewards to those of others. As a result of this comparison, they may feel equity or inequity; that is, they may feel that they are treated fairly or that they are not.

Everyone's contributions and rewards don't have to be the same for equity to exist. For equity to exist, people must perceive that the relative proportion of all rewards and all contributions is equal. And if equity is present, people are generally motivated to keep everything as it is. If individuals experience inequity, they are generally motivated to change something. This viewpoint suggests that individuals should be rewarded according to their contributions, which includes their performance as well as their knowledge and skills. Once you create a psychologically safe, equitable, or fair environment, individuals will be motivated to keep it that way.

Goals

Part of creating a psychologically safe environment is ensuring that individual goals are compatible with the organization's goals. Psychologically safe organizations should have the following shared goals: (1) encourage feedback; (2) active listening; (3) open communication; (4) admit vulnerability; and (5) build trust. The goal of creating psychological safety in the workplace is to make employees feel comfortable sharing their ideas, being themselves, and making mistakes without fear of judgment or retaliation. This can lead to increased collaboration, innovation, and overall team effectiveness.

Goal-setting theory suggests that goal-setting can be applied on an individual level as a way to increase employee motivation. The starting point is for group leaders and group members to meet regularly. As a part of these meetings, they should jointly set goals. These goals should be very specific and moderately difficult. Assuming they are also goals that the group members will accept and be committed to, they are likely to work very hard to accomplish them. Having clear goals is motivating for individuals.

Since future behavior is shaped by the consequences of current behavior, if people's current behavior leads to satisfactory results, they will likely engage in that same behavior in the future. But, if the current behavior does not lead to satisfactory results, or if that behavior leads to unpleasant results, the individuals are more likely to follow a different behavior pattern in the future.

Organizations are finding that when employees are given a greater voice in how things are done, those employees become more committed to the organization's goals and are willing to make ever-greater contributions to the organization's success. The use of this high-involvement approach is more than just participation, however. It involves a total approach whereby the organization's structure, processes, reward systems, and methods of doing the work are all altered to focus on information, knowledge, power, and rewards.

Ways and Schedules

A final question about motivation concerns how and why behaviors stay the same or change. What has happened? The answer probably involves reinforcement processes. The idea of reinforcement suggests that future behavior is shaped by the consequences of current behavior. If people's current behavior leads to a reward, they are likely to engage in that same behavior again. But if current behavior does not lead to a reward, or if it leads to unpleasant outcomes, they are more likely to follow a different behavior pattern in the future.

There are four basic ways to increase motivation: positive reinforcement, avoidance, extinction, and punishment. A reinforcement is anything the organization provides in exchange for services. Positive reinforcement is a reward, or desirable outcome, that is given after a particular desired behavior. Avoidance is aimed at avoiding negative consequences. It suggests that someone will repeat a desirable behavior in order to avoid an unpleasant situation. In extinction, nothing happens following a behavior; it is used to weaken behavior. The idea is that if poor behavior is ignored, it may go away, but this approach has many problems. Punishment, on the other hand, means that the behavior results in an undesirable consequence. Punishment is clearly used to discourage poor behavior, but again, this approach has many problems. However, the impact of these kinds of reinforcements on behavior is complicated by their schedule or the frequency with which the reinforcement occurs.

Positive reinforcement need not be given every time someone does the correct thing. Indeed, that could lead to the impact diminishing over time. Some form of regular but not continuous reinforcement will lead to individuals being motivated to continue to perform well because each incident raises the probability (though not the certainty) that the next will bring forth the reinforcement.

Obviously, if reinforcement is to lead to motivation, it must be effective. To be effective, it must first satisfy the basic needs of those in the organization. Second, it must be comparable to those offered by other organizations in the immediate area, and it must also be distributed fairly and equitably. Finally, the reinforcement must be multifaceted, which means that it must acknowledge that different people have different needs. A range of reinforcement must be provided, and people need to be able to attain rewards in different ways.

For reinforcement to be effective, organizations must know when to provide it. Five basic schedules of reinforcement are available: Continuous, fixed interval, variable interval, fixed ratio, and variable ratio. Consider each of them in turn.

Under the continuous reinforcement schedule, the reinforcement occurs after every occurrence of the behavior. Obviously, the power of the reinforcement will rapidly diminish since it is so common and easy to get.

Under a fixed interval schedule, the reinforcement occurs on a periodic basis, regardless of performance. However, since rewards do not affect performance, this is of limited value as a way to enhance motivation.

The variable interval schedule also uses time as a basis for reinforcement, but the time intervals between reinforcement vary. If rewards follow this schedule, it will tend to be powerful.

Under the fixed ratio schedule, reinforcement occurs on the basis of the number of behaviors rather than on the basis of time.

Finally, there is the variable ratio schedule, which is generally the most powerful one for enhancing motivation. Under this arrangement, reinforcement is given on the basis of behaviors, but the number of behaviors needed to get the reinforcement varies. The group member is motivated to continue to work hard because each incident raises the probability (though not the certainty) that the next will bring praise.

Obviously, if reinforcement systems are to serve their intended purpose, they must be effective. Effective reinforcement systems tend to have four basic characteristics. First, they must satisfy the basic needs of the group members. They must be adequate, reasonable, and appropriate. Second, the reinforcement must be comparable to those offered by other organizations in the immediate area. Reinforcements must also be distributed in a fair and equitable fashion. If they are not distributed in an equitable fashion, employees will be resentful. Finally, the reinforcement system must be multifaceted, which means that it must acknowledge that different people have different needs. A range of reinforcements must be provided, and people need to be able to attain them in different ways.

A reinforcer is anything the organization provides in exchange for services. Clearly, however, outcomes vary in terms of their potency as reinforcers. One category of reinforcers includes base pay, benefits, holidays, and so forth; these rewards are not tied to performance. A second category includes pay increases, incentives, bonuses, promotions, status symbols (bigger offices, reserved parking spaces), and attractive job assignments. These are reinforcers in the truest sense; they represent significant forms of positive reinforcement and satisfy many of the basic needs of most employees.

In summary, then, there are numerous kinds of reinforcers, both extrinsic and intrinsic. These include base pay, benefits, holidays, pay increases, incentives, bonuses, promotions, status symbols, praise, recognition, work assignments, and so on. To be an effective reinforcement system, four characteristics must be met: the system must satisfy basic needs, be comparable to those used elsewhere, be distributed equitably, and be multifaceted.

Having assured that others are motivated, now is the time for specifics regarding steps to develop a psychologically safe culture in your organization.

Case Study[1]

On his first day back after his training, the plant manager noticed a technical service technician in the lab having a discussion with an external contractor. While the technician was wearing safety glasses, the contractor was not. The manager has a no-tolerance policy as far as safety is concerned, and his normal response would be to call the technician to his office and, in his words, "read her the riot act."

(Continued)

Later, according to the manager's self-assessment: "*I am known to blow a fuse (or two) when safety rules are flouted; however, I managed to keep my cool and decided to test my training.*"

As a result, when he asked the technician to his office and saw that she was worried and even scared about his reaction, he changed tactics. Instead of leading with his dismay and disappointment, he started by explaining that he had just received some training on motivation. He shared key concepts of that training with her. He then asked her if she thought that the rule to wear safety glasses, even when there was no experiment being conducted, was "stupid" as there was no danger to the eyes. Did she feel imposed upon to wear safety glasses as she had no choice?

Since the technician was invited to have a discussion rather than "dressing down," she was open and candid. She explained that she had a two-year-old child, and she was extremely concerned about lab safety as she wanted to reach home safely every evening. To the manager's great surprise, she also shared that in certain areas, she would prefer even more, not less, stringent safety measures. For example, she suggested that safety shoes should be required for lab experiments that are conducted at elevated temperatures.

But when it came to wearing safety glasses when no experiments were being conducted, she just could not understand the rationale and did, indeed, resent the imposed rule. As a result, she didn't feel compelled to enforce it, especially with an external contractor. The manager said he understood her feelings and went on to provide the rationale that the intention was that wearing glasses would become a force of habit, just like wearing a safety belt in the car.

Case Questions

1. Is this a psychologically safe workplace? Why or why not? Try to be specific in your response.
2. Have you ever encountered an organization that had a rule or practice that you felt was wrong or unnecessary? How did you handle it? Be specific.

3. Identify some possible ways of preventing this problem. Again, be specific if you can do so.

4. What do you think about the manager's approach in this situation? Why?

Think About This Chapter

Take a few minutes to prepare responses to these questions and actions. Write your responses to help you remember them. In particular, if you are a manager, you should do this in order to be better prepared to achieve psychological safety in your organization.

Chapter Questions

1. What forms of reinforcers are used by your organization? Try to be specific in identifying them.

2. How/when are those reinforcers used by your organization?

3. Specifically, what changes in your organization's reinforcement systems would you suggest to make it more effective?

4. Can you identify different schedules of reinforcement in your organization? How effective do they seem to be?

Actions

Develop a plan of action to help your organization establish a more effective reinforcement system.

CHAPTER 6

Safety and Security

Safety applies with equal force to the individual, to the family, to the employer, to the state, the nation, and to international affairs. Safety, in its widest sense, concerns the happiness, contentment, and freedom of mankind.

—William M. Jeffers

Physical safety and security must also be addressed as part of attaining psychological safety. Organizations must ensure the safety and security of personnel and equipment, including protection from violence. If possible, hazards and security risks should be identified and eliminated (Cascio and Boudreau 2014, Bitsch and Olynk 2008, Bitsch et al. 2006, Van Fleet and Van Fleet 2007). Psychological safety contributes to a safer physical workplace by encouraging organization members to report potential hazards and safety issues. Efforts should be made to provide working conditions that are tolerable as well as safe (Bitsch and Olynk 2008, Bitsch et al. 2006). A safe environment tends to be one that is also relatively free from workplace violence.

Organizations find that implementing these following safety practices results in numerous benefits. Specifically, safety and health programs (www.osha.gov/safety-management):

- Prevent workplace injuries and illnesses;
- Improve compliance with laws and regulations;
- Reduce costs, including significant reductions in workers' compensation premiums;
- Engage workers;
- Enhance their social responsibility goals and;
- Increase productivity and enhance overall organizational operations.

To achieve health and safety goals, organizations need to plan ahead. Despite all of this, however, workplace violence incidents of one form or another may still occur. Thus, organizations must develop plans for emergency situations. Detailed contingency plans should be made, and a "crisis management team" identified that would be empowered to act when a violent incident occurs (Van Fleet and Van Fleet 2007).

To ensure the connection between a physically safe workplace and a psychologically safe one, an organization should (www.nsc.org/workplace/safety-topics/psychological-safety-correlates-to-physical-safety):

1. Support a psychologically safe workplace culture;
2. Encourage open communication;
3. Foster a learning mindset;
4. Be clear about expectations;
5. Support mental health and a recovery-ready workplace; and
6. Be supportive.

Various considerations are necessary to ensure physical safety, ranging from removing potential hazards to providing comfortable arrangements to avoid bodily stress and strain. While the specifics regarding these differ by industry or organization, risk assessments should be used to address conditions. A risk assessment is a procedure used to identify any real or potential hazards and analyze what could happen if a disaster or hazard occurs.

Risk assessments should be inclusive and cover everyone, including those who are disabled, females, and older members of the organization. To ensure that risk assessments are inclusive, organizations should ask everyone to identify their own safety risks and suggest any accommodations that may be needed to provide safe work environments.

There are five types of risk assessments: qualitative risk assessments, quantitative risk assessments, generic risk assessments, site-specific risk assessments, and dynamic risk assessments (www.evotix.com/resources/blog/5-types-of-risk-assessment-how-to-use-them). Qualitative assessments are cheaper and faster since they rely only on the judgments of one person. On the other hand, quantitative analysis relies on hard data and assigns percentages to indicate the possibility of it occurring or causing harm. Generic risk assessments assess a broad range of specific workplace activities and are most useful regarding repetitive tasks. Site-specific assessments pay attention to hazards that can only be found in one specific location. A dynamic risk assessment evaluates risks in rapidly changing, uncertain, and often high-risk environments. Conducting a risk assessment generally involves six stages:

1. Plan
2. Identify hazards
3. Evaluate identified risks
4. Take action
5. Record findings and actions taken
6. Review process

Workplace Safety[1]

The company should conduct annual inspections of all facilities as part of a worksite analysis. Such analyses are necessary to evaluate and determine any vulnerability to workplace violence or hazards. Corrective actions should be taken to reduce any and all risks identified. Security factors are a critical piece of the prevention process and include the assurance that deployed technology such as closed-circuit television cameras (CCTVs), access controls, doors, and locks are properly functioning. These components should be checked frequently, including emergency phones, emergency lighting, security escorts, panic buttons or switches, video monitoring, and metal detectors. Maintaining these safety and security devices helps to ensure a safe and violent-free workplace.

Of course, one of the first things an organization needs to do is to establish a health and safety policy. A well-developed policy may help the organization in accomplishing the following:

- Lay the foundation for controlling behavior;
- Dictate the resources that are required;
- Communicate management's commitment and direction;
- Provide direction to respond to abuse, intolerance, misconduct, and negative perception;
- Assist with legal action when the need arises;
- Protect the firm against scurrilous allegations;

- Help frame acceptable behavior;
- Clarify reporting procedures and;
- Establish response and investigative duties.

Before developing a policy for these situations, organizations should encourage the participation of everyone in the organization. Most importantly, the organization should assess behaviors that currently exist, as well as those that might develop in the future that could be perceived as violent or potentially violent.

In addition, identifying your organization's unique security aspects is important to providing a safe working environment. Area and items that are possible targets and vulnerabilities include:

- Medical products
- Military applications
- Clean water
- Food production
- Consumer products
- Telecommunications
- Automobile plants
- Warehousing
- Processing and production
- Buildings and offices
- Operations
- Process
- Infrastructure

Dangerous/Emergency Situations

While it is not always possible to positively identify all behaviors of perpetrators who might engage in workplace violence, there are certain behavior patterns that can serve as warning sign indicators of violence intervention. The following are some examples:

- Engages in sabotaging of equipment and/or intentionally damages property;

- Threatens suicide, actually destroys property, and vandalizes cars and personal property;
- Argues frequently, displays belligerence toward others, curses at co-workers, supervisors, customers, vendors, faculty, staff, and even students;
- Verbalizes wish or intent to harm you;
- Intimidates employees;
- Makes unwanted romantic approaches toward another employee;
- Is inclined to send violent notes, make harassing phone calls, make visual depictions, or send newspaper clippings of a designed message;
- Brags about possession of guns or at the extreme edge displays his weapon;
- Uses weapons or other dangerous objects to hurt you;
- Has committed homicide, sexual assault, arson, or physical assaults;
- Loner, socially isolated;
- Cannot accept criticism and holds grudges;
- Has an obsession with his job, but little to do with co-workers;
- Decreased attention to personal grooming;
- Involved with family, personal, or custody problems;
- History of being a victim;
- Engages in high-risk behavior;
- Increased absenteeism;
- Exhibits paranoid behavior;
- Extreme changes in behavior;
- Never assumes responsibility;
- Chronically disgruntled;
- Substance abuser;
- Obsessive interest in firearms;
- Recent experience of loss, shame, or humiliation;
- Bullying behavior;
- Externalizes blame;
- History of being violent;

- Suicidal tendencies;
- Stalking and harassing telephone calls and;
- Engages in physical confrontations and fights.

Shootings have received a lot of coverage in the media following the mass shooting at a light rail yard in San Jose; the Henry Pratt Shooting in Aurora, Illinois; shooting at Virginia Beach City Building; and the Walmart shooting in Southaven, Mississippi. Dobrilova (2021) presents some alarming statistics:

- Two million people become victims of workplace violence annually;
- Health care workers are most often affected—50 percent of cases involve medics;
- Seven percent of fatalities in the workplace involve some sort of physical damage;
- Women report around 30,000 sexual assaults on the job;
- About 60.4 million Americans have been bullied while working and;
- By April 2021, there were 26 victims of workplace shootings.

However, when an armed or dangerous individual is identified, he or she should not be confronted or encountered. You should not attempt to challenge or disarm the individual. Everyone should remain calm, make constant eye contact, talk to the individual, and notify security personnel. Such incidents must be reported for corrective action to be taken. If a person in charge can be safely notified of the need for assistance without endangering the safety of the employee or others, such notice should be given. Code words or hand signals can be used to communicate. Otherwise, cooperate and follow the instructions given by those involved to minimize the risk. The threat posed by an armed intruder is a reality and must be handled with care. Organizations should develop plans both as part of prevention and intervention for just these situations. Responding to threats involves organizationwide alerting, notifications, and communications capabilities, including evacuation, immediate protective measures, and the police response.

The S.A.F.E.T.Y. Model

The S.A.F.E.T.Y. model is one approach to attaining a physically and psychologically safe environment. As shown in Figure 6.1, it consists of six components—security, autonomy, fairness, esteem, trust, and you.

The six components have been presented in slightly different ways. Another presentation is that of Radecki, Hull, McCusker, and Ancona:

- Security—the need for predictability, consistency, commitment, certainty, (no) change;
- Autonomy—the need to feel that, as individuals, we have control over our environment and have choices;
- Fairness—the need to engage in and experience fair interactions both to us and to others;
- Esteem—the need to be regarded highly, derived from how we see ourselves and in comparison to how others think others see us;
- Trust—the social need to belong to and protect our in-group; and
- You—factors unique to you: your individual personality, your biases, how you are influenced, and your context (past, present, future) (Radecki, Hull, McCusker, and Ancona, 2018).

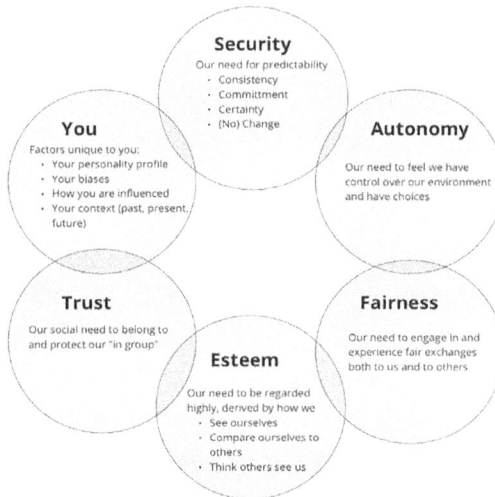

Figure 6.1 The S.A.F.E.T.Y. model

Source: https://unconsciousagile.com/2023/05/13/sagety-model.html.

While all of these needs are important to feel safe, they tend to exist on a continuum such that, at any given point in time, some are more important than others. Understanding which domain is most important to you will help you generate self-awareness around potential sources of stress and security. That awareness will assist you in determining what you can do to manage your safety to optimize your health and performance.

You should also learn from mistakes, how to work better and safer, reduce workarounds, and share knowledge when confidence is low (Edmondson, 2019).

Example

The following is an example of a workplace safety document from a major corporation.

Workplace Violence Prevention Policy/Plan

I. ***Purpose:*** *The [INSERT ORGANIZATION NAME] provides for a safe and secure workplace for all employees and affiliated partners (consultants, contractors, vendors, customers, and visitors) that is free of violence in the workplace and maintains a standard of zero incidence tolerance for all forms of incidents that may lead to violence. The purpose of this policy is to provide employees expectations and guidance that will help maintain [INSERT ORGANIZATION NAME]'S collective efforts at the headquarters, regional offices, and at all work-related events free of any recognizable or known hazards. The following specific objectives will be assured that:*

- o *A safe and healthy workplace is maintained;*
- o *Minimizes or eliminates violent behavior (e.g., verbal or physical aggression);*
- o *Minimizes the severity of injuries resulting from violent behavior;*
- o *Assures that employees exposed to violent behavior are provided appropriate medical care and counseling; and*
- o *Assures us that any employee making any such related report will be protected against retaliation.*

II. **Policy:** *[INSERT ORGANIZATION NAME] will maintain a zero-incidence tolerance standard against any forms of conduct by employees or nonemployees that might place personnel at risk consistent with this policy and as outlined by The Occupational Safety Health Act (OSHA). To manage and reduce the risk of violence, all employees should review and understand all provisions of this workplace violence policy, which includes customer/client violence, violence between employees, domestic violence and/or partner violence, and violence in connection with opportunistic criminal activity. This policy addresses any form of intimidation, harassment, direct or indirect threats of bodily harm (including written correspondence, email, and voice message), bullying, physical altercation (fighting, punching, jabbing, pushing, shoving, and assault) during a robbery at [INSERT ORGANIZATION NAME] headquarters, regional offices, and at sponsored events. Workplace violence will not be tolerated. The policy supports actions taken during a hostile intruder/ active shooter incident where imminent bodily harm is a consideration.*

III. **Background:** *Violent behavior of visitors and/or employees in [INSERT ORGANIZATION NAME] facilities and other locations where [INSERT ORGANIZATION NAME] employees are required to perform their duties is an occupational health hazard. Workplace violence is preventable, and most acts of violence in the workplace have warning signs (verbal and nonverbal). Prevention of violence in the workplace greatly enhances services provided by allowing staff to safely interact with visitors and other employees. Additionally, preventive measures reduce costs associated with work-related injuries.*

IV. **Definitions:**

    A. *Workplace Violence: Includes behavior in which an employee, former employee, or nonemployee inflicts or threatens to inflict serious bodily harm, injury, or death to others at the workplace or to inflict damage to property as a result of a business-related incident or condition. It includes behavior by employees, clients, customers, vendors, family, and visitors engaged in official business, at GMAC worksites or company sponsored events.*

    B. *Four (4) Different Categories of Workplace Violence: Type I—Violence in Connection to Robbery and Other Criminal Acts; Type*

II—*Customer/Client/Patient-Related Violence; Type III—Violence between Co-Workers, and Type IV—Domestic/Partner Relationship Violence Spilling Over to the Workplace.*

C. *Hostile Intruder/Active Shooter: A person or persons with a homicidal intent who enter the workplace in retaliation for the specific objective of harming or killing those he has targeted. The hostile intruder could be armed with a handgun, shotgun, machine gun, knife, or machete. This person typically has no intention of getting apprehended and will continue until he stops or is stopped by police.*

D. *Threat: The implication or expression of intent to inflict physical harm or actions that a reasonable person would interpret as a threat to physical safety or property.*

E. *Physical Assault: Push, shoving, kicking, spitting, fighting, or armed robbery.*

F. *Intimidation: Making others afraid or fearful through threatening behavior.*

G. *Domestic/Intimate Partner Violence Workplace Spillover: Abusive behavior between parties and their association to the workplace and its explosive potential to cause co-workers and others in the affected area to be placed at risk.*

H. *Verbal Abuse: Making profane or antagonizing remarks in an attempt to annoy, anger, harass, or intimidate.*

I. *Harassment: Making any profane or antagonizing remarks to attempt to annoy, anger, harass, and impede movement and/or any act involving nuisance phone calls, emails or written correspondence, or annoying pranks to include intimidation.*

J. *Zero-Incident Tolerance: A standard that establishes that any behavior, implied or actual, that violates the policy will not be tolerated.*

K. *Exception to the Zero-Incident Tolerance Policy is an encounter with a hostile intruder/active shooter where there's a decision to incapacitate the individual by any actions taken by the employee in mitigating risk to others.*

L. *Court Order: An order by a court that specifies and/or restricts the behavior of an individual or organization. Court orders may be issued in matters involving domestic violence, stalking, or harassment, among other types of protective orders, including temporary restraining orders.*

M. *Examples of Prohibited Conduct: Violence in the workplace may include, but is not limited TO, the following list of prohibited behaviors directed at or by a co-worker, supervisor, or member of the public: [INSERT ORGANIZATION NAME] will not tolerate any type of workplace violence committed by or against employees. Affiliated supervisor or manager will complete a Workplace Violence Incident Report Form. The supervisor/manager shall inform the security program manager/human resources to assess, evaluate, and discuss the need for intervention by local law enforcement officials, the objective is prevention of escalation of any act of violence. Employees who have a restraining order, temporary or permanent, against an individual due to a potential act of violence, who would be in violation of the order by coming near them at work, shall immediately supply a copy of the signed order to their supervisor/ manager. The employee's supervisor/manager of the affected area shall provide copies of the report to their immediate manager, security program manager and director of human resources.*

V. **Enforcement:** *The policy addresses reporting requirements, supervisory responsibility, incident response, assessment, and investigation relative to any form of workplace violence noted earlier. Any employee determined to have willfully violated this policy will be subject to disciplinary action, up to and including termination and criminal prosecution. Nonemployees who engage in such behavior on [INSERT ORGANIZATION NAME] property, by telephone, voice mail, email, or other forms of correspondence directed against any [INSERT ORGANIZATION NAME] employee, affiliated partner or customer will be reported to a supervisor or manager immediately, asked to leave the premises and (depending on the circumstances or if they cease to desist) reported to the proper law enforcement authorities and if arrested prosecuted to the full extent of the law.*

VI. **Responsibilities:** *All employees have a duty and responsibility to report all incidents to their immediate supervisor/manager so as not to place others at potential risk. The supervisor/manager receiving an employee complaint or report is to document the complaint or report and immediately notify their direct manager and/or director of human resources to determine what necessary action should be taken to resolve and prevent the situation and/or incident from escalating. At risk situations* *involving a serious threat of bodily harm will be coordinated with the security program manager. [INSERT ORGANIZATION NAME] will investigate all complaints filed and will also investigate any possible violation of this policy by [INSERT ORGANIZATION NAME] personnel or others. In the event of an imminent threat to personnel safety, the security program manager shall be notified of the details immediately by the swiftest means possible. If desired, the employee filing such a report will be notified of the findings but not necessarily the disciplinary action. In case of imminent bodily harm, the intended victim (s) will be kept informed to include notification of appropriate police agencies should the need determine doing so. In addition, the Violence Response Team will conduct a threat assessment to determine risk and apply the best risk minimization measures.*

a. *Management Response Team:*

    1. *[INSERT ORGANIZATION NAME] has established an incident response team that is responsible for the overall implementation and maintenance of [INSERT ORGANIZATION NAME] Workplace Violence Prevention Plan. Management Response Team (MRT) members are management level representatives from the following departments:*

        o *Human resources*
        o *Security program manager*
        o *Risk management*
        o *Crisis management*
        o *Corporate council*
        o *Resource center management*
        o *Safety management*
        o *Corporate council*
        o *EAP*

    2. *The MRT's duties include, but are not limited to, improving [INSERT ORGANIZATION NAME]'s readiness to address workplace violence by:*

        o *Reviewing past incidents of violence and contributing factors.*
        o *Reviewing [INSERT ORGANIZATION NAME]'s readiness to respond to issues of workplace violence.*

- o *Developing an expertise among MRT members and other appropriate members of management regarding issues of workplace violence prevention and assessment.*
- o *Establishing liaison with local law enforcement and emergency services.*
- o *Training [INSERT ORGANIZATION NAME] personnel.*

3. *Establishing and maintaining policies and procedures for dealing with issues of workplace violence among affiliated partners and temporary personnel.*

4. *The MRT may assign all or some of these tasks to other individuals within the company. Nevertheless, the MRT remains ultimately responsible for implementing and maintenance of [INSERT ORGANIZATION NAME]'s Workplace Violence Prevention Plan.*

5. *Managers and supervisors shall be responsible for the following:*
   - o *Workplace violence prevention training for personnel under their supervision.*
   - o *Assisting MRT with implementing and maintaining the workplace violence program.*
   - o *Managers, supervisors, and all employees shall be held accountable for reporting all incidents and following up on violence-related reports.*

VII. *All [INSERT ORGANIZATION NAME] personnel shall obey all approved workplace violence prevention policies.*

VIII. ***Incident Reporting Requirements:*** *It is every [INSERT ORGANIZATION NAME] employee's responsibility to report any personnel security threats that have the potential for placing others at risk. You must not assume that [INSERT ORGANIZATION NAME] is aware of the specific situation and condition. All incidents, situations, and conditions must be reported immediately to a supervisor/manager and the director of human resources for assessment and evaluation. A serious life-threatening situation is to be reported directly to the security program manager. An incident involving an immediate threat by a hostile intruder/active shooter must be reported immediately under the Safe Harbor Room and Violence Response Procedures and Plans. Employees are encouraged to report personnel, situations, or conditions that place others at risk anonymously or for attribution (on the* *record). Regardless of the origin of the report a Workplace Violence Incident Report must be completed. All reported incidents would be assessed, evaluated, and given appropriate investigative attention. Reports or incidents warranting independent of engaging the security program manager and/or human resources. Managing risk factors is the responsibility of [INSERT ORGANIZATION NAME] supervisors/managers in coordination with the MRT. Supervisors/managers must remain vigilant and proactive in their recognition of potential at risk personnel, situations, or conditions that may lead to escalation and workplace violence. Remember, the objective is to identify any at-risk person, situation, or condition in preventing escalation and resolving disputes to prevent escalation. Therefore, supervisors/managers will monitor their workplace settings to include the [INSERT ORGANIZATION NAME] property and community settings to assess potential security threats. All employees must not assume that a customer elevated dispute that's momentarily resolved should go unreported. All incidents must be reported and documented.*

- o *Hostile Intruder/Active Shooter: In the event of a hostile intruder/active shooter incident or any individual possessing any type of weapon intending to inflict eminent bodily harm on [INSERT ORGANIZATION NAME] premises or in shared workspace and buildings, follow the protocols and procedures outlined in the Safe Harbor Room and Hostile Intruder Response Procedures. In addition, specific instructions shall be provided to all employees pertaining to their unique environments related to workplace security and potential hazards unique to their workplace settings.*

b. *Domestic Violence/Intimate Partner Violence Workplace Spillover: While often originating in the home, it can significantly impact workplace safety and the productivity of victims as well as co-workers. For the purposes of this document, "domestic violence/intimate partner violence" is defined as abuse committed against an adult or fully emancipated minor. Abuse is the intentional reckless attempt to cause bodily injury, sexual assault, threatening behavior, harassment, or stalking, or making annoying phone calls to a person who is in any of the following relationships: Spouse or former spouse; Domestic partner or former domestic partner; Cohabitant or former cohabitant and or other household members; a person with whom the victim is having, or has had a dating or engagement relationship; a person with whom the victim has a child. Such at-risk situations can significantly impact workplace safety and security if prevention and protective measures are not in place. For the purposes of this document personnel are to advise their supervisor/manager when they feel they are in a potentially violent relationship and if, and when a court order has been issued against their spouse or intimate partner relationship. Employees who are aware of an at-risk domestic or intimate partner relationship situation are encouraged to report their observations and concerns immediately. Such reports can be made anonymously and/ or treated confidentially. Employees who request assistance will be provided an appropriate level of care and attention to confidentially. However, in situations of extreme urgency involving death threats of hostile intruder confidential information will be handled in the best interest of workplace safety and security.*

IX. ***Worksite Assessment or Analysis and Employees at Risk:*** *Supervisors/managers should have a familiarity with their employee's permanent and temporary worksites, settings, and customer/client relationships, and should be aware of potential at-risk situations and conditions. The worksite assessment or analysis serves as an ongoing oversight of and early warning of impending need for intervention and interdiction. The worksite assessment provides the workplace violence prevention policy and security function an opportunity to stay abreast of potential problems, offering assistance, addressing situations, and resolving conflict. The primary purpose of the worksite assessment or analysis is to identify potential at-risk situations before they become workplace threats. Supervisor/managers will coordinate efforts with the director of human resources in providing assistance to at-risk employees and victims of workplace violence. Employees affected by workplace violence will receive the support and assistance through the director of human resources. The security program manager, in cooperation with the department manager, will design a risk minimization or safety plan if the need determines such actions necessary. Risk minimization can include a report to the police, change of* *schedule or relocation depending on the nature of the employee's expo-sure and situation and even environmental configuration of office set-tings. While [INSERT ORGANIZATION NAME] does not expect employees to be skilled in identifying all potentially dangerous per-sons or situations, employees are expected to exercise good judgment in reporting their observations and reports to their immediate supervisor/manager. The security program manager is responsible for conducting annual inspections of the premises as part of the worksite analysis to evaluate and determine any existing security gaps and potential work-place hazards. The worksite assessment will consist of quality assurance and examination of the working conditions of CCTVs, access controls, (doors, locks, badges), visitor management, emergency evacuation are identified, emergency alert, communication, and notification system properly functions and that all emergency response procedures and pro-tocols are current. Department managers should be involved in the annual worksite-specific analysis and assessment.*

X. ***Incident Investigation:*** *In the event of an actual reported inci-dent, noninjury or hostile intruder threat, the primary objective is to respond and conduct as thorough as possible a fact-finding post incident investigation of the circumstances leading up to the threat or assault, record and report the observations, findings and recommen-dations, and conduct a threat assessment. Personnel reporting obser-vations and encounters must do so immediately by the fastest possible means. When filing a reported act of workplace violence that does not involve a serious injury or a hostile intruder threat do the fol-lowing: interview the participant (victim(s) and perpetrator); iden-tify and interview witnesses; visit the scene of the incident as soon as possible; determine the cause of the incident; provide medical care for minor injuries, provide a supervisory escort for medical services, take mitigating action to protect victims and witnesses who have safety and security concerns; and record and report findings. If appropri-ate, [INSERT ORGANIZATION NAME] will inform the reporting individual of the results of the investigation. To the extent possible, [INSERT ORGANIZATION NAME] will maintain the confiden-tiality of the reporting employee and the investigation, but may need to disclose results in appropriate circumstances; for example, in order* *to protect individual safety or when disciplinary action is pending. [INSERT ORGANIZATION NAME] will not tolerate retaliation against any employee who reports an incident of workplace violence.*

XI. ***Threat Assessment:*** *The primary objective of the threat assessment process is hasty intervention to manage, reduce, and prevent escalation through early intervention and identify any at-risk personnel, contributing factors and recommending risk abatement measures. In the event of a serious threat of bodily harm to an employee or affiliate partner, the assessment will attempt to determine capability, opportunity, and circumstances to quickly assess the need for immediate protective measures to include the need for relocation, temporary employment reassignment, and police intervention. All personnel who make observations and encounters must file a report immediately. All incidents will be reported to the employee's immediate supervisor/ manager who will complete the Workplace Violence Incident Report Form and provide the original to the security program manager and/ or the human resource director (Violence Response Team). However, regardless of the incident, a preliminary assessment shall take place to identify early intervention measures. The MRT will be activated to take appropriate steps in protecting employees and others. Emergency threats will be reported to the police.*

XII. ***Crisis Management/Communications Management:*** *Crisis Management/Communications Management will serve as the [INSERT ORGANIZATION NAME]'s spokesperson. When police and other emergency organizations arrive on the scene, their principal objective will be information gathering. The objective of Communications is sharing pertinent information and information management to avoid premature disclosures and serve as the bridge between the media, first responders, emergency personnel, and government agencies.*

XIII. ***Terminations:*** *Since the success of [INSERT ORGANIZATION NAME]'s workplace violence prevention efforts is predicated on multiple intervention strategies, decisions to terminate an employee, contractor, or consultant should not be taken lightly and certainly not in a vacuum. Therefore, every effort should be made to be thoughtful, considerate, and empathetic. Set the tone appropriate to the situation, delivered with professionalism. Create an environment where the* *employee fully accepts his or her responsibility without any personal domination to ensure a safe and secure transition. The objective is to eliminate the need for a police or uniform security presence. When the security presence is required, coordinate the deployment with the security program manager. Do allow the employee ample time during the process to ask questions and offer observations. If possible, consider the employee's recommendations for improved employee–management relationships. Avoid engaging the employee in argumentative discussions at this time. If there is a conflict between the terminated employee and the manager initiating the termination, that supervisor or manager should not be involved in the termination proceedings to the extent possible. Establish the parameters for the meeting early on. Ensure that the setting is identified and prepared in advance, and that everything the employee is promised is delivered immediately including his/her separation disbursements and explanation of related entitlements. While the termination proceeding should promote a spirit of understanding, remaining firm and professional is the ultimate outcome. Never allow others not part of the immediate process to offer commentary during the meeting or at any time following the termination. Keep a watchful eye out for indicators of disgruntled tendencies and be prepared to intervene early to avert disaster. It is essential to understand that the employee controls his thoughts, his intentions, and his actions. Don't create an emotional contagion by assuming that the termination is the solution to the immediate problem. Always treat the employee with dignity and respect during and after the termination. Plan the termination to be a continuous process without interruptions so that the situation will not allow the employee who may be thinking of retaliation to return as a hostile intruder. Control the process until the employee has left the building.*

XIV. ***Training Management:*** *Training should consider content and the audience. Training for the sake of training is fruitless and counterproductive. The content must be audience specific and tailored to a specific need and supporting a workplace violence prevention strategy. Avoid mixing the audiences with employees and supervisors and managers for the purpose of expedient scheduling. All employees who missed scheduled training should be reprogrammed. The training value is derived when there is a combination of lecture, group discus-*

sions, and other activities. The training should focus on the preven-
tion of violence in the workplace in the employee's unique workplace
setting and consider the four categories of workplace violence (Type I,
II, III, and IV). Key to the success of workplace violence prevention
training is a review of the [INSERT ORGANIZATION NAME]
workplace violence, firearms, misconduct, and active shooter policies
and procedures. Past incidents can serve as content for mini-incident
discussion for supervisors and managers. Greater training value can be
maximized if supervisors and managers suggest training content.

XV. ***Training and Instruction****: The Training and Development Depart-*
ment in coordination with the human resource director, security
program manager, and department directors shall be responsible for
ensuring that all employees, including managers, supervisors, and
security and safety personnel are provided adequate training and
instruction on aspects of workplace violence prevention and violence
response. Department directors shall be responsible for scheduling all
employees, including supervisors and supervisors to attend training
and receive worksite-specific instructions. Department managers are
also responsible for rescheduling missed training opportunities for
all employees in their departments. The training content will serve
to reinforce the Workplace Violence Prevention Policy and Plan, the
Safe Harbor Room, Violence Response Procedures, Evacuation Drills,
and other standing security measures intended to improve emergency
readiness.

a. *Training and instruction shall be provided as follows:*
   o *To all current employees when the policy is first*
     implemented.
   o *To all newly hired employees, supervisors, and managers, or*
     employees.
   o *To employees involved in a workplace violence incident*
     who might request additional training.
   o *To all consultants and contractors engaged in long-term*
     projects with the company.

b. *Workplace Violence Prevention and Security Training and Instruc-*
   tions will include, but is not limited to the following:
   o *Explanation of this Workplace Violence Prevention Policy.*
   o *Aspects of workplace violence prevention.*

      o *Reporting procedures for reporting incidents and situations.*
      o *Conflict management and methods to de-escalate hostile or threatening situations.*
      o *Safe Harbor Room and Shelter in Place/Immediate Protective Measures.*
      o *Hostile intruder/active shooter violence response.*
      o *Emergency evacuation procedures.*

XVI. ***Hiring and Retention Considerations****: While the human resource department takes reasonable measures to conduct background investigations to review candidate's backgrounds to reduce the risk of hiring individuals with a history of violent-prone behavior, changes in settings, circumstances, personal behavior away from the workplace, personal situations and attitudes change in people over time. Supervisors and managers are expected to exercise care and concern in being observant of increasingly alarming employee behavior changes and reports of concerning circumstances.*

XVII. ***Leadership Challenges****: Supervisors and managers should strive to exercise responsible supervision. Employees should be treated fairly with dignity and respect. The disciplinary process should be devoid of personal inferences and kept professional throughout the proceedings. Disciplinary proceedings are not "get even" opportunities. Where possible, employee representatives should be allowed to participate in the disciplinary process unless specific legal reasons exist prohibiting such practices. Discourage supervisors from drawing premature conclusions about the employee or situation until all the facts are in. Refrain from the public display of favoritism for employees or trying the disciplinary outcome in public. Handle and respond to all employee complaints and reports immediately and appropriately. Keep the employee informed and respond to any follow-up information requested or provided during or after the incident.*

XVIII ***Conclusion****: The [INSERT ORGANIZATION NAME] provides for a safe and secure workplace for all employees, contractors, consultants, vendors, and visitors that is free of violence in the workplace and maintains a standard of zero incidence tolerance for all forms of incidents that may lead to violence. Workplace violence prevention is an organizational responsibility and a management commitment.*

Case Study[2]

Carolinas HealthCare System (CHS) is the largest health care system in the Carolinas and the third largest nonprofit public health care system in the nation. CHS owns, leases, or manages 29 hospitals in North and South Carolina and employs more than 1,400 physicians practicing in more than 500 locations. CHS also operates rehabilitation hospitals, nursing homes, ambulatory surgery centers, home health agencies, radiation therapy centers, and physical therapy facilities. Together, these operations comprise more than 6,000 licensed beds and employ more than 44,000 full-time or part-time employees.

The health system's employee health department used a manual system for tracking, recordkeeping, and reporting. The size of the organization and the number of separate locations and departments required stacks of forms for many critical programs. Beyond consuming significant resources, the manual approach also meant slow turnaround times and potential for human error throughout the process. CHS wanted to automate medical surveillance tracking, simplify reporting, and ultimately give employee health department staff the best possible tools to do their jobs efficiently and effectively. But other variables had to be considered as well, including cost and the inevitable challenges of implementation, training, and upgrades when dealing with large organizations.

Case Questions

1. Is the CHS a psychologically safe organization? Why or why not? Be specific.
2. What might be the pros and cons of some sort of automated system? Think about this from the viewpoints of the organization, the employees, and the clients.
3. Would adopting an automated system make CHS more or less psychologically safe? Explain your response.
4. Would an automated system help or hinder communication at CHS?

Think About This Chapter

Take a few minutes to prepare responses to these questions and actions. In particular, managers should do this to be better prepared to achieve psychological safety in their organizations.

Chapter Questions

1. What forms of risk assessment are used by your organization? Try to be specific in identifying them.
2. Does your organization follow all of the steps in the S.A.F.E.T.Y. model?
3. Specifically, are there areas where your organization should be more concerned about safety?
4. Does an organization have to be safe to also be psychologically safe?

Actions

Develop a plan of action to help your organization become a physically safe place to work.

CHAPTER 7

Approaches

Success depends on psychological safety. At Google, members of teams with high levels of psychological safety were less likely to leave their jobs, brought in more revenue, and were rated effective twice as often by executives. MIT researchers who studied team performance came to the same conclusion: simply grouping smart people together doesn't guarantee a smart team. Online and off, the best teams discuss ideas frequently, do not let one person dominate the conversation, and are sensitive to one another's feelings.

—Liz Fosslein

Numerous approaches have been suggested for developing psychological safety. Among some of the more widely known approaches are the Four Stages, the Five Pillars, and the Playbook. Those interested in any of these specific approaches should consult the cited references to learn more about the particular approach. However, by way of introductions, brief summaries of each of them are presented here.

Four Stages[1]

Building on the basic concept of psychological safety as discussed in the opening chapter (psychological safety occurs in organizations in which conditions are nonthreatening, predictable, and in which members could engage one another), the four stages refer to conditions in which individuals feel (1) included, (2) safe to learn, (3) safe to contribute, and (4) safe to challenge the status quo. True psychological safety occurs when all four stages exist.

Stage 1—Inclusion Safety

The first stage involves the individual's need to be included, accepted, and belonging. Being adopted and accepted in the group is the first step in feeling psychologically safe. Individuals need to interact and be true to themselves. More importantly, they need to feel safe and that they won't risk making a mistake or challenging the status quo. They step outside of their comfort zones and volunteer to take on more responsibility.

Stage 2—Learner Safety

The second stage involves the individual's need to learn and grow on the job. When there is learner safety, group members are not afraid to ask each other questions, try new things, experiment, and make mistakes. They need to be able to make mistakes as part of the learning process. Thus, rather than being punished, mistakes are rewarded as part of the learning process. This stage involves both formal learning experiences and the individual's own informal learning experiences.

Stage 3—Contributor Safety

Here, the individual's need for autonomy is involved. Contributor safety is the stage where individuals may fully employ their skills and expertise. Respect must be shown for the individual's contributions. Guided autonomy rather than complete freedom is involved. Roles are clearly defined, but individuals are expected to think outside of their roles. On the other hand, individuals must be accountable for their efforts.

Stage 4—Challenger Safety

In the final stage, individuals need to be free to innovate and suggest ways to improve existing organizational procedures. On the other hand, rather than making specific suggestions, individuals at this stage may simply question the way of doing things but should feel free and, indeed, protected in doing so. This stage allows for the creative dissent that is needed

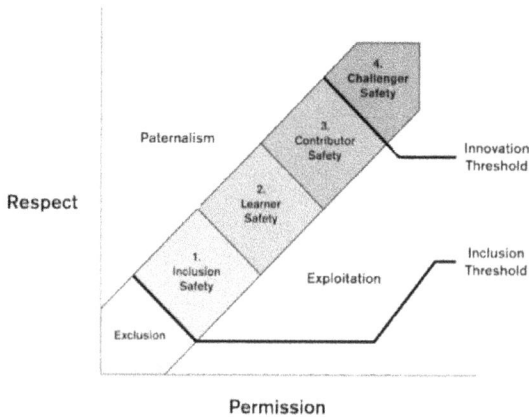

Figure 7.1 Four stages of psychological safety

Source: Adapted from https://psychsafety.co.uk/the-four-stages-of-psychological-safety/.

for innovation. Group members should not fear retaliation or any risk to their positions within the organization.

> To create a truly inclusive and psychologically safe environment, organizations must integrate and prioritize all four stages. Each stage builds upon the previous one, creating a progression that nurtures a culture of psychological safety from its foundation. By recognizing the interconnectedness of these stages, organizations can ensure that psychological safety becomes an integral part of their values, practices, and norms.

(www.leaderfactor.com/). Consider the way(s) that your organization needs to make in order to move from whatever stage it is into one closer to Challenger Safety.

Five Pillars*

The five pillars approach is intended to be implemented through training programs offered by Gina Battye. As shown in Figure 7.2, it involves

---

* This section is based on the work of Gina Battye at www.ginabattye.com/5-pillars-psychological-safety/.

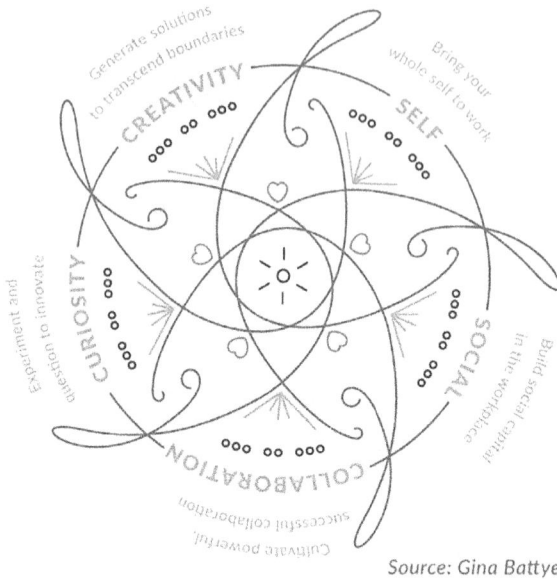

Source: Gina Battye

Figure 7.2 The five pillars

five "pillars" that provide the support for the emergence of psychological safety when all five become embedded within an organization.

The pillars then are (1) self—bring your whole self to work; (2) social—build social capital in the workplace; (3) collaboration—cultivate powerful and successful collaboration; (4) curiosity—experiment and question to innovate; and (5) creativity—generate solutions to transcend boundaries. Briefly, each of them can be described as follows.

Pillar 1—Self

Here, the individuals must be themselves at work. They must be self-aware. In developing that self-awareness, they have to ask themselves what affects their performance, what they can do about it, and their personal goals. This self-awareness enables each individual to be more confident, to inspire those around them, and to make a fuller and lasting contribution to the organization.

Pillar 2—Social

This pillar involves the social network in the organization, specifically patterns of communication. Again, the individual must ask themselves questions about how they communicate with others, especially how their messages are received and how their communication might be improved. As communication improves, individual relationships are enhanced, and greater understandings are achieved among not just those within the organizations but also customers, suppliers, and all stakeholders.

Pillar 3—Collaboration

Building on improved communication, this pillar involves developing successful collaborative arrangements within the organization. The concern is to develop conditions where everyone can develop and be better members of the organization. Goals must be identified or clarified, and each person's role and contribution must be clarified. This opens the way for improved innovation and processes in the organization.

Pillar 4—Curiosity

This pillar involves experimentation and innovation. Learning and development are key components of this pillar. Individuals must feel safe to make mistakes and try new and different ways of working together. The improved innovation developed in Pillar 3 is further developed and sustained. Both performance and productivity see improvements as this pillar is fully embedded.

Pillar 5—Creativity

This pillar completes the support structure as a transformative shift in individual problem-solving and creative thinking occurs. Individuals generate solutions that go beyond existing boundaries. Problem-solving becomes paramount. Individual engagement with the organization is maximized, as are their contributions. Overall, organization performance in terms of goal attainment is enhanced, whether the goal be revenue, profit, or customer service at nonprofit organizations.

The Psychological Safety Playbook[2]

Another approach to developing psychological safety in an organization involves a unique technique—using plays or vignettes to stimulate the reader's thinking. These are presented in a short little book, the size of which should not diminish its potential impact. There are five short plays or vignettes. Those five plays are: (1) communicate courageously, (2) master the art of listening, (3) manage your reactions, (4) embrace risk and failure, and (5) design inclusive rituals. Each play begins with a short vignette illustrating a point followed by five "moves" or issues designed to cause the reader to examine his or her reactions to the play and the point being made.

The authors suggest that you experiment with the Playbook in group discussions and individually. They argue that even using one move will make a big difference to an organization. Briefly, here are the five plays and the moves associated with them. Note that while the moves are sketchily presented here, you should obtain a copy of the book to understand each of them more fully.

Communicate Courageously

This play begins with a vignette about an engineer who communicates in a way that encourages others to become involved. Then, five "moves in this play" are presented to involve the reader in analyzing the vignette. Those moves include: (1) welcoming other viewpoints, (2) soliciting diverse perspectives, (3) expressing your own emotions, (4) taking off the mask of perfection, and (5) nurturing a sense of humor at work.

Master the Art of Listening

The vignette in this play involves the head of a bank visiting the branches of the bank. The moves in this vignette are: (1) listen to understand, (2) be fully present, (3) clarify your understanding, (4) listen for emotions, and (5) commit to curiosity.

Manage Your Reactions

Here, the vignette describes a meeting in which a colleague modeled how to handle strong reactions. The moves are then: (1) model nondefensive reactions, (2) respond productively, (3) watch out for your blind spots, (4) appreciate being challenged, and (5) build on others' ideas.

Embrace Risk and Failure

The vignette describes an individual's reflection on how a client was aided to develop a growth mindset for the organization. The moves are: (1) normalize failure, (2) reframe failures as learning opportunities, (3) get comfortable with discomfort, (4) model learner behavior, and (5) celebrate continuous learning.

Design Inclusive Rituals

The final vignette is a recollection of an inclusive leader. The moves in this last vignette are: (1) upgrade meetings, (2) respect all voices, (3) take turns, (4) check for psychological safety, and (5) appreciate the team.

Summary

As noted earlier, numerous approaches have been suggested for developing psychological safety. The ones presented here are among the most widely known. Hopefully, you will use the works cited to explore each of them. However, you are especially encouraged to use the one presented in the next chapter, the V-REEL framework.

Case Study[3]

Imagine being in Ms. Rishika's shoes. As a sales manager, she was entrusted with the responsibility of securing critical orders for her company. However, a fateful day arrived when she lost a substantial order worth 10 million rupees due to a seemingly minor delay in submitting a revised quote. The repercussions of this loss were dire, and Rishika faced a dilemma.

Instead of disclosing the real reason for the order loss, she recorded in the customer relationship management (CRM) system that the client had chosen a competitor due to their "higher prices." Rishika's decision to conceal the truth was driven by an overwhelming fear of disclosing her mistake and the potential negative consequences

---

(Continued)

> that might follow. Unfortunately, this decision ultimately led to her downfall.
>
> Several months later, a sales analyst conducted a thorough analysis of the situation and unearthed an astonishing revelation. The competitor had secured the order by quoting a price that was a whopping 20 percent higher than Rishika's offer.

Case Questions

1. Is this a psychologically safe organization? Why or why not? Be specific.
2. What caused Rishika to hesitate to share the reason for the order loss? Who is responsible for Rishika's false reporting about the reasons for the order loss? Think about this both from her viewpoint and that of the organization.
3. What might be done in order to move the organization closer to being psychologically safe? Be specific.
4. Are you aware of anyone in your organization "hiding" mistakes?

Think About This Chapter

Take a few minutes to prepare responses to these questions and actions. In particular, managers should do this to be better prepared to achieve psychological safety in their organizations.

Chapter Questions

1. Is your organization using one of these approaches?
2. If your organization is not using one of these, what is it doing? Try to be specific in identifying the approach used.
3. Specifically, are there areas where your organization should be more concerned about psychological safety?
4. Can you identify any of the pillars in your organization? Be specific.

Actions

Develop a plan of action to help your organization become a psychologically safe place to work.

CHAPTER 8

V-REEL[1]

For us at Deitz Consulting, the most powerful components of the V-REEL framework are to look at things from the perspective of erosion or eroding factors and enabling factors. It helps us as a team look at what could come into the market and cause us to falter or fail. What things might chip away at our customer base and hurt them and us?

—Deitz Consulting, Texas

The recommended approach to achieving psychological safety is to use The V-REEL framework. That framework was originally developed by Dr. David Flint (2018) as a guide to assist organizations in thinking through what they know (and need to know) about their resources and capabilities to assess the organization's potential for creating value in their environment. It has been modified as an approach for developing psychological safety in organizations.

Flint's book, *Think Beyond Value*, presents the V-REEL framework, a framework that he originally developed to aid his teaching of strategy formulation. Since developing the tool, Flint has used V-REEL in support of consulting engagements, and is now working to use it with both his for-profit and not-for-profit enterprises domestically and internationally. *Think Beyond Value* describes the V-REEL framework in an easy-to-read and practical manner, and is sure to be a valuable resource to any organization or individual seeking to think beyond value and develop sound strategy for business and for life.*

Not only a professor, Dr. Flint is also a businessman, consultant, public speaker, and now, an author. Outside of professional endeavors, Dr. Flint

---

* This and the next paragraph are from www.seadgallery.com/2018/04/author-talk-with-david-flint/.

finds joy in dog walking, music, and traveling the world. Throughout his career, Dr. Flint has been involved in management ranging from start-up companies to real estate investment. Presently, he holds board and leadership positions across business endeavors in software applications, real estate, and insurance. He has also helped to create two nonprofit organizations and now serves on the board for both organizations with domestic and international activities. When Dr. Flint is not teaching strategic management and entrepreneurship at Texas A&M, he enjoys public speaking and consulting.

The V-REEL letters as used here should be interpreted as follows:

- **V** indicates value. In this case, it is the value of having a psychologically and physically safe workplace. Achieving a high value is clearly what is to be desired. This includes value to everyone in the organization as well as to suppliers, customers, and all stakeholders.
- **R** indicates the rareness of that value. Few organizations have truly achieved completely psychologically and physically safe workplaces. It is important to consider why it is rare in your organization. Why is it rare?
- **E**—the first E indicates factors, forces, conditions, policies, or behaviors that might erode (E) or chip away at your ability to create value, that is, psychologically and physically safe workplaces. What are those things in your organization that are keeping your organization from becoming psychologically safe?
- **E**—the second E indicates factors, forces, conditions, policies, or behaviors that enable (E) or help to create that value. What things in your organization could you change or improve to help your organization become psychologically safe? How will you go about identifying them?
- **L** indicates longevity, how long you have to obtain the value before it is too late, and how long you might expect the value to last. Realistically, it would help to consider how long it will take to obtain psychological safety and how long it will last before things change and it diminishes.

Value and Rareness

As indicated in previous chapters, the value of psychologically, psychosocially, and physically safe workplaces has clearly been established. Both psychological and psychosocial safety are needed in not just work organizations but in all organizations (Lennox 2021). Psychological safety impacts numerous aspects of the organization, including employee well-being, retention rates, creativity, employee engagement, and collaboration (Cooper 2023). A psychosocial safety climate has been shown to positively impact work engagement and job performance (Idris, Dollard, and Tuckey 2015). It has also been shown to reduce presenteeism or the lost productivity occurring when employees are not fully functioning at work because of an illness, injury, or other condition (Mansour et al. 2022). Physical safety has been shown to result in reduced absenteeism, higher-quality production, more motivated and competent workers, as well as reductions in replacement and training costs (Thiede and Thiede 2015). In 2017, the cost of work injuries was $161.5 billion, and the cost per worker was $1,100, which included the value of goods or services each worker must produce to offset the cost of work injuries (AmTrust Financial 2019). According to a more recent survey, companies receive a return on investment of $3 or more for each $1 they spend to improve workplace safety (Mlynek 2021).

Jiménez (2022) indicates that the benefits of psychological safety include:

- Enhanced employee engagement;
- Encouragement of creativity and new ideas;
- Improved employee well-being;
- The creation of brand ambassadors;
- Reduced employee turnover;
- Boosted team performance; and
- Fostering an inclusive workplace culture.

Furthermore, an inclusive culture provides a high sense of belonging and can result in as much as a 50 percent reduction in employee turnover.

Unfortunately, despite the benefits, psychological and physical approaches to safety at work are relatively rare (Scorza 2018). A 2023 survey found more females (23%) than males (15%) reported a toxic workplace; those living with a disability (26%) reported a toxic workplace more than those without a disability (16%); and upper managers were much less likely to report a toxic workplace (9%) than those in middle (21%) or front-line workers (26%) (MacArthur 2023).

Eroding Factors

Eroding factors are forces, conditions, policies, or behaviors that might erode or chip away at your ability to create value, that is, a psychologically and physically safe workplace. They harm your ability to create value. Lists of eroding factors can be quite lengthy. Some of the more obvious ones are the following:

- Arguing—with co-workers, managers, customers, or anyone else leads to time away from productive endeavors.
- Backstabbing—those who belittle your work, steal your ideas, take credit where it isn't due, point fingers, start rumors, or shirk responsibility all detract from the quality of the workplace.
- Bad lighting—leads to eye strain, headaches, poor posture, accidents, injuries, poor mental health, and emotional well-being.
- Bigotry—unreasonable beliefs or disliking others impairs working relationships.
- Bullying—Praslova et al. (2022) indicate that about 30 percent of the workforce is bullied at work, severely damaging productivity.
- Dictatorial leadership—managers never listen, they have no empathy, they have "chips" on their shoulders, they demand that things be done their way, and in other ways behave so as to detract from a good organizational culture.
- Drinking—before going to work and while at work both pose significant problems for organizations.
- Empire-building—this form of politically motivated behavior detracts from the primary objectives of the organization.

- Favoritism—leads to pitting one member of the organization against another and is clearly damaging to the development of a spirit of cooperation.
- Gossiping—malicious, untrue talk about someone or the organization detracts from the goals of the organization and can damage the relations among people in the organization.
- Harassment—whether verbal, psychological, physical, or sexual, all forms of harassment are unacceptable in the workplace.
- High turnover—means some individuals are new and just learning about the work and the organization, so they are not as productive.
- Inadequate space utilization—employees lacking the space and resources necessary to do their best work are less productive.
- Inconsistent messaging—individuals are told to do X but also that the organization expects Y, and other forms of mixed messages only serve to confuse people and decrease performance.
- Lack of accountability—blaming others for mistakes, not following through on commitments, and avoiding responsibility, all lead to negative consequences for the organization.
- Lack of collaboration—"when people choose to work together, they experience a significant increase in their intrinsic motivation" (Stefirta, n.d.), so if you do not have collaboration, motivation suffers.
- Lack of safety concern—obviously, if no one is concerned about safety, you will not get safety.
- Leader refuses responsibility for errors—when managers dodge responsibility, so will others, resulting in an increase in errors.
- Outdated technology—can lead to frequent crashes in processes, dangers in cybersecurity, and compliance issues, among other problems.
- Overemphasis on leader's success—the leader/manager may benefit but at the expense of the organization's performance.
- Poor benefits—could lead to poor performance, high turnover, and difficulties finding quality replacements.

- Poor customer service—not only can your reputation be damaged, but you stand to lose customers and your best employees.
- Poor workplace culture—no clear core values and norms not clearly defined or communicated, leading to confusion and ambiguity and decreased performance.
- Poor workplace hygiene—leads to stress, illness, decreased morale, and damaged organizational reputation.
- Preferential treatment—like favoritism, this leads to pitting one member of the organization against another and is damaging to the development of a spirit of cooperation.
- Prejudice—similar to bigotry, having attitudes or stereotypes about others can lead to discord among members of the organization.
- Saying one thing, meaning another—another form of inconsistent messaging.
- Sexual comments—have no place at work and are likely to increase bullying and harassment.
- Spreading rumors—wastes time, damages reputations, promotes divisiveness, creates anxiety, and destroys morale.
- Swearing—has no place at work and could lead to damaged cooperative relations.
- Taking drugs—has no place at work, can damage cooperative relations, and involve the organization in unwanted publicity and/or legal action.
- Toxic culture—this would be the worst case of a poor culture.
- Turf wars—competition between parts of the organization that is likely to promote divisiveness, create anxiety, and destroy cooperation.
- Yelling—loud, angry arguments are unacceptable; they are disrespectful, embarrassing, unprofessional, uncomfortable, and detract from a cooperative, productive environment.

Now is the time to use the five W and one H questions. Why, Who, What, Where, When, and How. Why is it necessary to try to reduce or eliminate them? Who should be or is responsible for each eroding factor? What should or can be done about them? Where should you begin to try to reduce or eliminate them? When should you begin? And finally, how should you act to reduce or eliminate them?

As you think about answers to these questions, remember that "Rome wasn't built in a day." All of these can't be corrected at once. You should prioritize your efforts and note that others may be easier to achieve once one or two have been corrected. But before tackling these eroding factors, consider focusing on enabling factors, as using them may actually assist in correcting one or more of the eroding ones.

Enabling Factors

Identifying factors or forces that could be useful in bringing about psychological safety is not as clear-cut. Different writers have made various suggestions, which are not always supported by hard evidence. Most of the suggestions focus on leaders or managers; nevertheless, examining those would be helpful.

Attfield (2019) suggests that leaders should:

- Break the "Golden Rule";
- Welcome curiosity;
- Promote healthy conflict;
- Give employees a voice;
- Earn and extend trust;
- Promote effectiveness, not efficiency; and
- Think differently about creativity.

Barnett (n.d.), on the other hand, advises leaders to:

- Show your team you're engaged;
- Let your team see you understand;
- Avoid blaming to build trust;
- Be self-aware—and demand the same from your team;
- Nip negativity in the bud;
- Include your team in decision making;
- Be open to feedback; and
- Champion your team.

Bosler (2021) argues that psychological safety is a key component for achieving diversity, equity, and inclusion, and suggests that leaders should:

- Promote self-awareness;
- Demonstrate concern for team members as people;
- Actively solicit questions;
- Promote positive dialogue and discussion;
- Be precise with information, expectations, and commitments;
- Provide multiple ways for employees to share their thoughts;
- Show value and appreciation for ideas;
- Explain reasons for change; and
- Own up to mistakes.

Edmonson and Hugander (2021) have a simpler list and note that leaders should:

- Focus on performance;
- Train both individuals and teams;
- Incorporate visualization; and
- Normalize vulnerability related to work.

The National Association of Safety Professionals (NASP, 2023) suggests that organizations take these steps:

- Create a positive and supportive culture;
- Prioritize training and onboarding;
- Have clear policies for bullying and harassment;
- Adjust employee workspaces;
- Foster supportive leadership through training;
- Construct strong lines of communication;
- Facilitate career development;
- Provide staff with psychosocial safety training;
- Host team building events;
- Identify psychosocial hazards;
- Assess the risks and prioritize;

- Implement risk control measures; and
- Monitor and review.

O'Donohoe and Kleinschmit (2022) feel that leaders should:

- Evaluate and set explicit norms and expectations;
- Model vulnerability;
- Remember, everyone has a unique perspective;
- Be a transparent communicator;
- Create a culture of appreciation; and
- Get to know your team.

Ravishankar (2022) states that organizational leaders should:

- Not fixate on building a "perfect" team;
- Allow the team to make mistakes;
- Avoid placing blame when things go wrong;
- Recognize and reward people when things go right;
- Encourage diversity, equity, and inclusion;
- Understand and support diversity;
- Check their own biases;
- Build cultural competence;
- Communicate with care;
- Be vulnerable; and
- Show empathy.

Tiwari and Lenka (2016) have a somewhat different set of recommendations. They suggest that organizations:

- Provide opportunities for members to share their ideas by having regular meetings, brainstorming sessions, and a database available to everyone.
- Encourage employees to raise concerns and express appreciation when they do.
- Encourage employees to contribute their thoughts and expertise.

- Develop a program for continuous learning by organizing workshops, conferences, and seminars, and by encouraging members to accept challenging assignments and to furnish the necessary infrastructure, resources, and financial support to accomplish this.
- Provide opportunities for members to take risks and be intrapreneurs by providing flextime and allowing failures while they attempt risky projects.

Wegner (n.d.) suggests that the leaders of the organization should:

- Establish an open and respectful communication culture;
- Be transparent in order to build trust;
- Set clear expectations;
- Reframe failure and mistakes as opportunities for learning and growth; and
- Take a supportive and consultative approach to leadership.

There are 17 general concepts among these enabling factors. Those concepts are the following (Van Fleet 2024):

1. Blame—Avoid blaming to build trust; avoid placing blame when things go wrong; earn and extend trust; nip negativity in the bud.
2. Clarity—Set clear expectations; have clear policies for bullying and harassment; be precise with information, expectations, and commitments; incorporate visualization.
3. Communication—Communicate with care; construct strong lines of communication; establish an open and respectful communication culture; explain reasons for change.
4. Concern—Demonstrate concern for team members as people; let your team see you understand; adjust employee workspaces.
5. Discussion—Promote positive dialogue and discussion; promote healthy conflict; monitor and review.
6. Diversity—Encourage diversity, equity, and inclusion; understand and support diversity.
7. Innovation—Welcome curiosity; think differently about creativity.

8. Involvement—Actively solicit questions; be open to feedback; encourage employees to contribute their thoughts and expertise; encourage employees to raise concerns and express appreciation when they do; give employees a voice; provide opportunities for members to share their ideas by having regular meetings, brainstorming sessions, and a database available to everyone; provide multiple ways for employees to share their thoughts; include your team in decision making.

9. Learning/training—Train both individuals and teams; prioritize training and onboarding; develop a program for continuous learning by organizing workshops, conferences, and seminars, and by encouraging members to accept challenging assignments and to furnish the necessary infrastructure, resources, and financial support to accomplish this; facilitate career development; host team-building events; provide staff with psychosocial safety training; build cultural competence.

10. Mistakes—Allow the team to make mistakes; reframe failure and mistakes as opportunities for learning and growth; own up to mistakes.

11. Performance—Focus on performance; promote effectiveness, not efficiency; evaluate and set explicit norms and expectations.

12. Risk—Assess the risks and prioritize; implement risk control measures; provide opportunities for members to take risks and be intrapreneurs by providing flextime and allowing failures while they attempt risky projects.

13. Self-awareness—Be self-aware and demand the same from your team; check your own biases; promote self-awareness.

14. Support—Create a positive and supportive culture; foster supportive leadership through training; take a supportive and consultative approach to leadership; create a culture of appreciation; champion your team; recognize and reward people when things go right; show value and appreciation for ideas.

15. Transparency—Be a transparent communicator; be transparent in order to build trust.

16. Understanding—Get to know your team; remember that everyone has a unique perspective; show empathy; show your team you're engaged.

17. Vulnerability—Be vulnerable; model vulnerability; normalize vulnerability related to work.

Here again, ask the Why and Who questions. Why is it necessary to try to develop these? Who should be or is responsible for such development? What should or can be done to develop them? Where should you begin to try to develop them? When should you begin? And finally, how should you act to develop? As with the eroding factors, think about your answers and prioritize your actions. As you achieve one or more of these, reducing eroding factors should be easier, and some momentum will build you toward achieving psychological safety.

Longevity

In order to fully implement psychological safety, you and your organization must strive to adopt each and every one of these "themes." When all of these are adopted, the organization will be in Stage 4 and will likely remain that way for some time, although getting there will likely be a long and arduous journey.

With turnover, new members may cause one or more of the eroding factors to again come into play, and changes in the environment could also lead to a falling back on those factors. "To ensure the longevity of the value thus obtained, the enabling factors "must become institutionalized and systematized" (Edmondson 2018 82). The perceptions of others in the organization will not all align with one another, so you need to recognize, acknowledge, and address each and every person. Individuals must be able to safely bring their own thoughts, perceptions, and experiences to the organization. You then should use different steps to bolster, rebuild, or reinforce psychological safety within the organization (Loignon and Wormington 2022, 15). In this way, longevity will be maintained.

Final Results

A careful use of the V-REEL framework will help you and your organization achieve psychological safety. But remember that psychological safety is "a never-ending and dynamic journey" (Edmondson 2018, 103).

"Psychological safety at work *doesn't* mean that everybody is nice to each other all the time. It means that people feel free to 'brainstorm out loud, voice half-finished thoughts, openly challenge the status quo, share feedback, and work through disagreements together—knowing that leaders value honesty, candor, and truth-telling and that team members will have one another's backs" (Center for Creative Leadership 2023). "Psychological safety isn't about being nice. Nor is it about constantly agreeing with one another for the sake of avoiding hurt feelings" (Anonymous 2020).

Clark (2021) says, "Psychological safety is not a shield from accountability. It's not niceness, coddling, consensus decision-making, unearned autonomy, political correctness, or rhetorical reassurance."

Geraghty (2023) indicates that psychological safety is not:

- About **lowering standards;**
- **Specifically about mental health**, well-being, or wellness;
- **Synonymous with job security;**
- **A permanent state;**
- **Solely dependent on leadership**, nor is it only the group's responsibility;
- **Linked to certain personalities;**
- **Trust;**
- **About pretending everything is fine;**
- **An excuse for brutality;**
- **A peripheral concern**, or a "nice to have";
- **Intangible;** and
- Comfortable, particularly for people in leadership roles.

Psychologically safe environments exist when members of the organization share the belief that "they will not be exposed to interpersonal or social threats to their self or identity, their status or standing, and to their career or employment when engaging in learning behaviors such as asking for help, seeking feedback, admitting errors or lack of knowledge, trying something new or voicing work-related dissenting views" (Kaloudis 2019). Qualls and the CultureAlly Team (2022) identify interpersonal or social threats as rejection, disrespect, and intimidation, being labeled unfavorably or receiving a punishment that impacts the person's identity, status, and/or career. The environment you are trying to achieve is one in which it is possible to learn from mistakes and collectively avoid making the same mistakes in the future, a psychologically safe environment.

Case Study[2]

Mark and Bethany Douglass each run businesses and are well-practiced at employing the V-REEL framework. Mark leads operations for Fidelis Creative Agency, a creative design business he runs with his brother, Tim Douglass. Bethany runs a popular lifestyle blog, Cloistered Away, which focuses on purposeful living. However, they use the V-REEL framework as a tool for long-term family life. They've been adapting the V-REEL framework to their family life.

The L in V-REEL, Longevity, helps them carry out their family mission statement—training their children in an atmosphere that seeks creativity, education, and fosters the entrepreneurial spirit in their kids. Bethany is quick to point out that as a family, they apply V-REEL to more than business/financial decisions. It also works with abstract and emotional goals and helps the kids better understand who they are. When something comes up, she's able to say, "Let's talk about how you're responding to the circumstance. How it's working for you and how it's working against you."

Case Questions

1. Would using the V-REEL framework likely result in a psychologically safe family environment? Why or why not?
2. What eroding or enabling factors might the Douglass family encounter?
3. How might this use of the V-REEL framework lead to other applications?
4. Would you consider using V-REEL framework for your family situation?

Think About This Chapter

Take a few minutes to prepare responses to these questions and actions. In particular, managers should do this to be better prepared to achieve psychological safety in their organizations.

Chapter Questions

1. How valuable would psychological safety be for your organization?
2. What eroding factors exist in your organization?
3. What enabling factors exist in your organization?
4. Have you used the V-REEL framework to better understand how and why certain behaviors are associated with dysfunctional organizations? I would love to hear from you. Send comments to Dr. David D. Van Fleet (comments. dr.vanfleet@gmail.com).

Actions

Use the next chapter for a final check.

CHAPTER 9

How to Foster Psychological Safety in Your Group

A lot of what goes into creating a psychologically safe environment are good management practices—things like establishing clear norms and expectations so there is a sense of predictability and fairness; encouraging open communication and actively listening to employees; making sure team members feel supported; and showing appreciation and humility when people do speak up.[1]

A careful and detailed use of the V-REEL framework will help you and your organization achieve psychological safety. So, your first priority is to concentrate on its use. It is also important to demonstrate engagement, show understanding, be inclusive, and show confidence without being inflexible.

Use the V-REEL Framework

You may find it beneficial to print the lists of eroding and enabling factors provided here or, if you prefer, develop your own lists unique to your organization. Keep the lists with you or at your workplace to constantly remind you to avoid the eroding factors and adopt the enabling ones.

1. Determine your value.
   Get input from all employees, managers, and nonmanagers to assess the value of psychological safety to your organization. The value should be determined by including everyone in the organization, as well as suppliers, customers, and all stakeholders.

2. In what way is it rare?

As with determining value, be sure to get input from all employees, especially females, disabled employees, and all levels of management, in determining why it is rare in your particular organization. Consider that it may not align with the current organizational culture and, as such, not really be considered by managers, especially the highest-ranking ones.

3. Identify eroding factors and reduce or eliminate them. Remember that eroding factors are forces, conditions, policies, or behaviors that might erode or chip away at your ability to create value, that is, psychologically and physically safe workplaces. Which of the following things in your organization keep your organization from becoming psychologically safe?

   o Arguing
   o Backstabbing
   o Bad lighting
   o Bigotry
   o Bullying
   o Dictatorial leadership
   o Drinking
   o Empire-building
   o Favoritism
   o Gossiping
   o Harassment
   o High turnover
   o Inadequate space utilization
   o Inconsistent messaging
   o Lack of accountability
   o Lack of collaboration
   o Lack of safety concern
   o Leader refuses responsibility
   o Outdated technology
   o Overemphasis on leader's success
   o Poor benefits
   o Poor customer service
   o Poor workplace culture

- o Poor workplace hygiene
- o Preferential treatment
- o Prejudice
- o Saying one thing, meaning another
- o Sexual comments
- o Sexual touching
- o Spreading rumors
- o Swearing
- o Taking drugs
- o Toxic culture
- o Turf wars
- o Yelling

4. Identify enabling factors and adopt or increase them. Remember that enabling factors are forces, conditions, policies, or behaviors that enable or help to create that value. Which of the following are present in your organization?

- o Avoid placing blame when things go wrong;
- o Set clear expectations;
- o Have clear policies for bullying and harassment;
- o Be precise with information, expectations, and commitments;
- o Construct strong lines of communication;
- o Establish an open and respectful communication culture;
- o Explain reasons for any changes that need to be made;
- o Demonstrate concern for group members as people;
- o Adjust employee workspaces;
- o Promote positive dialogue and discussion;
- o Encourage diversity, equity, and inclusion; understand and support diversity;
- o Welcome curiosity;
- o Actively solicit questions;
- o Be open to feedback;
- o Encourage employees to contribute their thoughts and expertise and to raise concerns;
- o Express appreciation when they do;
- o Include your group in decision making;
- o Train both individuals and groups;

- o Develop a program for continuous learning;
- o Facilitate career development;
- o Host group-building events;
- o Provide staff with psychosocial safety training;
- o Allow the group to make mistakes;
- o Reframe failure and mistakes as opportunities for learning and growth;
- o Own up to mistakes;
- o Focus on performance;
- o Promote effectiveness, not efficiency;
- o Evaluate and set explicit norms and expectations;
- o Assess the risks and prioritize;
- o Implement risk control measures;
- o Provide opportunities for members to take risks and be intrapreneurs;
- o Provide flextime and allow failures while they attempt risky projects;
- o Be self-aware—and demand the same from your group;
- o Check your own biases; promote self-awareness;
- o Create a positive and supportive culture;
- o Foster supportive leadership through training;
- o Create a culture of appreciation;
- o Recognize and reward people when things go right;
- o Be a transparent communicator;
- o Remember everyone has a unique perspective; show empathy;
- o Show your group you're engaged;
- o Be vulnerable.

5. Determine your time frame.

Remember that changing conditions or personnel will necessitate refocusing on preventing or decreasing the eroding factors and introducing or encouraging the enabling factors.

In addition to using the V-REEL framework, there are other steps that you should take to achieve psychological safety. Some of these overlap the enabling factors (or decrease the eroding ones) and may already have been accomplished when you use the V-REEL framework. Those steps include the following.

Demonstrate Engagement

- Declare that you want feedback.
- Be present and focus on the conversation (e.g., close your laptop during meetings and turn off your cell phone).
- Ask questions to learn from your groupmates.
- Offer input, be interactive, and show you're listening.
- Respond verbally to show engagement ("That makes sense. Tell me more." "I hear you loud and clear.")
- Be aware of your body language; make sure to lean toward or face the person speaking.
- Make eye contact to show connection and active listening.
- Remember the 6 C's of employee engagement. They are Compliance, Clarification, Confidence, Connection, Culture, and Checkback.

Show Understanding

- Recap what's been said to confirm mutual understanding/ alignment (e.g., "What I heard you say is…"); then acknowledge areas of agreement, disagreement, and be open to questions within the group.
- Validate comments verbally. ("I understand." "I see what you're saying.")
- Avoid placing blame ("Why did you do this?") and focus on solutions. ("How can we work toward making sure this goes more smoothly next time?" and "What can we do together to make a game plan for next time?")
- Think about your facial expressions—are they unintentionally negative (a scowl or grimace?).
- Destigmatize failure.
- **Reframe failure and mistakes as learning opportunities**.
- Nod your head to demonstrate understanding during conversations/meetings.
- Express gratitude.

Be Inclusive in Interpersonal Settings

- Share information about your personal work style and preferences, and encourage groupmates to do the same.
- Be available and approachable to groupmates (e.g., make time for ad hoc one-on-one conversations, feedback sessions, career coaching).
- Communicate the purpose of ad hoc meetings scheduled outside normal meetings.
- Express gratitude for contributions from the group.
- Step in if group members talk negatively about another group member.
- Have open body posture (e.g., face all group members, don't turn your back to a part of the group).
- Build rapport (e.g., talk with your groupmates about their lives outside of work and socialize with them).

Be Inclusive in Decision Making

- Acknowledge input from others (e.g., highlight when group members were contributors to a success or decision).
- Connect with employees (but be sensitive).
- Don't interrupt or allow interruptions (e.g., step in when someone is interrupted and ask him/her to repeat the information to ensure that his/her idea is heard by everyone).
- Explain the reasoning behind your decisions (live or via email, walk the group through how you arrived at a decision).
- Focus on inclusive recruitment strategies.
- Give employees multiple ways to provide feedback.
- Invite participation by opening the conversation with "What am I missing?" "Catch me up."
- Provide safe spaces for employees.
- Solicit input, opinions, and feedback from your groupmates.
- Start from the top.

Show Confidence and Conviction Without Appearing Inflexible

- Embrace power poses.
- Encourage everyone in your group to take risks and demonstrate risk-taking in your own work.
- Hold an assertive posture.
- Invite those in your group to challenge your perspective and push back with ideas of their own.
- Maintain eye contact.
- Manage group discussions (e.g., don't allow side conversations in group meetings, make sure conflict isn't personal).
- Model vulnerability; share your personal perspective on work and failures with your groupmates.
- Pay attention to your facial expressions.
- Support and represent the group (e.g., share the group's work with senior leadership, give credit to groupmates).
- Use a voice that is clear and audible in a group setting.
- Walk into the room with self-confidence.
- Watch your hands.

You will probably not be able to employ all of these suggestions at any one time, but you should strive diligently to employ as many as you possibly can as quickly as you can to achieve psychological safety. Remember that tiny steps are for tiny people; take large steps instead.

Examples From Organizations[2]

Google

Google's mission is to "bring the best of Google to help solve some of humanity's biggest challenges—combining funding, innovation, and technical expertise to support underserved communities and provide opportunity for everyone" (www.google.org/). To do so, it connects innovative nonprofits and social enterprises with its own resources to accelerate their impact. Google uses "20 percent time" to foster psychological safety. This "time" is when employees are encouraged (but not required) to work on side projects that fall *outside* of their normal work assignments.

NASA

The National Aeronautics and Space Administration (NASA) is an independent agency of the U.S. government. As of 2022, it had over 18,000 employees. Then, after its space shuttle disintegrated while reentering the Earth's atmosphere, killing all seven people on board, NASA instituted challenger safety when it formed the Safety Culture program to allow the NASA community to voice safety concerns without fearing any repercussions. With this program, members can feel safe to disagree with one another or even management, or they can suggest something different.

Buffer

Buffer started in November 2010 and is self-described as "an optimistic and gratitude-filled group of remote workers scattered around the world and dedicated to creating a product our customers will use and love" (https://buffer.com/about). Initially, it had a Bootcamp for new members, but in 2017, Buffer did away with Buffer Bootcamp because they had come to realize that this probationary period was having a negative impact on their team's psychological safety. If new employees feel insecure or cautious for their first six weeks, the organization will miss out regarding their candid thoughts and risky ideas.

Unqork

Enterprise software company Unqork tries to assist others in building and managing enterprise-grade software without having to write their own code. It works to empower businesses to create, secure, and maintain the entire life cycle of their applications. To achieve inclusion safety, Unqork operationalizes diversity, equity, and inclusion by having it be part of their interview process. During interviews, interviewers ask questions to ensure that those hired are being bought into safe spaces for everyone, regardless of their ethnic or racial background. Unqork also hosts monthly trust-and-respect-building sessions for managers to help further create an inclusive culture.

Oak9

Oak9 is a software as a service (SaaS) company that analyzes and integrates existing ways in which the sequence of industrial, administrative, or other processes of organizations operate from beginning to end. As such, it operates remotely from numerous locations. Micromanagement tends to occur where more remote teams exist. In these situations, managers may overcompensate for a lack of trust by micromanaging the team members they cannot see. To prevent this and establish contributor safety, the cloud security company oak9 has a practice of establishing clear goals. New organization members discuss projects and goals for their first 30, 60, and 90 days, and each department clearly communicates the end goal for all projects.

Achievers

Achievers uses an employee recognition program to empower its employees. Its employee recognition platform involves pulse surveys, frequent check-ins, and networks to help organizations achieve the best from their members. Achievers has created inclusion safety by offering various employee resource groups (ERGs), which help employees feel that they belong and develop connections based on their different life experiences. These ERGs range from those with specific identities (and those who support them), such as the women's ERG, to specific interests, such as the wellness ERG.

Case Study[3]

I once was in charge of running the social media channels for the company I worked for. When I shared a post to the company's Instagram channel, one of my colleagues would often make a sarcastic remark or roll their eyes. They would comment on little details, from the choice of words to the choice of images.

(Continued)

Their constant criticism made me feel anxious and self-conscious about my work. I started questioning whether I was doing a good job. I second-guessed every post, trying to anticipate every possible criticism and making sure that everything was perfect. I felt paralyzed by the fear of making a typo or facing more snide comments.

As these small criticisms accumulated, I increasingly felt like I couldn't take any risks or be creative in my work. I was so afraid of being criticized or judged that I started playing it safe, putting up bland and uninspired posts that wouldn't draw attention or invite any criticism. The more my psychological safety eroded, the more my work suffered.

Case Questions

1. Is this organization a psychologically safe one? Why or why not? Be specific in your response.
2. Have you ever encountered an organization that made you anxious or self-conscious about your performance? How did you handle it? Be specific.
3. Identify possible ways of preventing or rectifying this problem. Again, be specific.
4. Is fear a major obstacle to obtaining psychological safety? Why or why not?

Think About This Chapter

Take a few minutes to prepare responses to these questions and actions. In particular, managers should do this to be better prepared to achieve psychological safety in their organizations.

Chapter Questions

1. What forms of enabling factors exist in your organization? Try to be specific in identifying them.
2. What forms of eroding factors exist in your organization? Try to be specific in identifying them.

3. Specifically, what changes in your organization's policies, practices, or behaviors would you suggest to make it more psychologically safe?

4. Have you used the V-REEL framework to better understand how and why certain behaviors are associated with dysfunctional organizations? I would love to hear from you. Send comments to Dr. David D. Van Fleet (comments. dr.vanfleet@gmail.com).

Actions

Develop a plan of action to help your organization establish a more effective reinforcement system.

Sources Specific to This Chapter

Edmondson, A. C. 1999. "Psychological Safety and Learning Behavior in Work Groups." *Administrative Science Quarterly* 44 (2): 350–83.

Edmondson, A. C. 2019. *The Fearless Organization.* Hoboken, NJ: John Wiley & Sons.

Edmonson, A.C., and Z. Lei. 2014. "Psychological Safety: The History, Renaissance, and Future of an Interpersonal Construct." *Annual Review Organizational Psychology and Organizational Behavior* 1: 23–43.

Flint, D. 2018. *Think Beyond Value—Building Strategy to Win.* New York, NY: Morgan James Publishing.

Goman, C.K. 2011. *The Silent Language of Leaders: How Body Language can Help—or Hurt—How You Lead.* Hoboken, NJ: Jossey-Bass Publishing, April.

Helbig, K, and M. Norman. 2023. *Psychological Safety Playbook.* Vancouver, B.C: Page two.

Rigby, A. 2024. "Real-Life Examples Proving Psychological Safety Is Crucial." https://getmarlee.com/blog/psychological-safety.

CHAPTER 10

A Cautionary Note

Is it possible to have too much of a good thing? Can there be too much psychological safety in an organization? As more organizations have achieved or made significant progress toward achieving psychological safety, some issues have occurred (Carbajal 2024; Howatt 2024; Jansen 2021). Short-term performance could suffer if too much time is used for innovation or for dealing with criticisms from organizational members (Eldor, Hodor, and Cappelli 2023; Eldor and Cappelli 2024; Weinstein, 2023). Of course, open communication about these effects should off-set them (Maximo, Stander and Coxen 2019; Clark 2022). However, in organizations with substantial external rules and regulations, such as sports organizations, psychological safety will necessarily be curtailed to some degree (Taylor, Collins, and Ashford 2022). Remember that psychological safety is a learning process aimed at long-term organizational success. There is no one-size-fits-all solution. Organizations must tailor their interventions to suit the unique needs and dynamics of their workforce (National; Safety Council n.d.).

As one final suggestion, consider adopting the Humanist's Guide.

A Humanist's Guide for Managers[1]

1. Focus on the goals of the organization rather than your personal goals.
2. Ask questions to be certain that you understand all communications.
3. Do not bully, harass, or otherwise abuse others in the organization.
4. Treat everyone fairly and ethically regardless of race, gender, age, creed, identity, orientation, physical ability, or status.
5. Analyze situations carefully. Use reason as your guide. Science, knowledge, observation, and rational analysis are the best ways to determine any course of action.

6. Do not insist that yours is the only and correct way.

7. Manage with reason, not with tradition or superstition.

8. Whenever possible, be kind in dealing with others.

9. Be careful with resources and their use.

10. Teach, instruct, and guide others so that everyone will learn and improve.

Appendix

Helpful Organizations

- American Society of Safety Engineers
  520 N Northwest Highway
  Park Ridge, IL 60068
- Association of Threat Assessment Professionals
  808 R ST STE 209
  Sacramento, CA 95811
- Bureau of Indian Affairs
  MS-4606
  1849 C Street, NW
  Washington, DC 20240
- Equal Employment Opportunity Commission
  131 M Street, NE
  Washington, DC 20507
- Federal Communications Commission
  45 L Street NE
  Washington, DC 20554
- Human Rights Watch
  350 Fifth Avenue, 34th Floor
  New York, NY 10118-3299
- International Association for Healthcare Security and Safety
  2005 Bloomingdale Rd
  Glendale Heights, IL 60139
- Occupational Safety and Health Administration
  200 Constitution Ave NW
  Washington, DC 20210

- U.S. Bureau of Labor Statistics
  Postal Square Building
  2 Massachusetts Avenue NE
  Washington, DC 20212-0001
- U.S. Department of Health and Human Services
  200 Independence Avenue, SW
  Washington, DC 20201

Glossary[1]

Everyone, but especially managers, should be familiar with these terms.

It would be useful to copy these for reference, especially in meetings or group discussions.

360-Degree feedback: Feedback is obtained from an employee's subordinates, peers, colleagues, and supervisor, as well as a self-evaluation by the employee themselves is gathered.

AA: Affirmative action.

Abjection: The separating of an individual from the group through statements of disgust.

Absenteeism: Intentional or habitual absence from work.

Abuse: Any action that intentionally harms or injures another person.

Acceptable Use Policy (AUP): A policy that defines computer and network users' responsibilities and appropriate behavior.

Accommodation: Making special circumstances for someone.

Accountability: Answerability for actions, decisions, and performance.

Activate: To make active; cause to function or act.

Active Shooter/Hostile Intruder Threat: A person or persons with a homicidal intent who enter the workplace in retaliation for the specific objective of killing those he has targeted. The Hostile Intruder could be armed with a handgun, shotgun, machine gun, knife, or machete. This person typically has no intention of getting apprehended and will continue until he stops or is stopped by police.

ADA: Americans with disabilities.

ADD: Administration on developmental disabilities.

ADEA: Age Discrimination in Employment Act.

AFAB and AMAB: Acronyms meaning "assigned female/male at birth" (also designated female/male at birth or female/male assigned at birth).

AFDC: Aid to Families with Dependent Children.

Affect: An emotion that changes or influences what you do or think.

Affected area: This is the general space or area where the unrestrained hostile intruder is roaming until contained.

Affirmative action: Plans of action undertaken by organizations to comply with human rights legislation by actively striving to recruit, hire, train, develop, and promote women and members of minority groups.

Affirmed gender: The gender by which one wishes to be known.

Age discrimination: Discrimination based on age; see also discrimination.

Agent: A person who acts for or in the place of another person.

Aggravation: A source or cause of annoyance or exasperation.

Aggressive: Pursuing one's aims and interests forcefully, sometimes unduly so.

Aggressor: A person who says or does hurtful things.

Aggrieved person: Someone who has been discriminated against in some way.

Agreeableness: The tendency to get along with other people.

AIDS: Acquired immunodeficiency syndrome.

Ally: A person who helps or stands up for someone who is being bullied or the target of prejudice.

Ambiguous information: Information that can be interpreted in multiple and often conflicting ways.

Anger-related incidents: Sudden display of aggression, impulsivity, or disruptive behavior.

Antibias: A commitment to avoid prejudice, stereotyping, and all forms of discrimination.

Antisocial: Not sociable; not wanting the company of others.

Anxiety: A feeling of worry, nervousness, or unease, typically about an imminent event or something with an uncertain outcome.

Apology: A regretful acknowledgment of an offense.

Arbitrator: A labor law specialist paid jointly by the union and the organization to listen to both sides of a labor dispute and then decide how the dispute should be settled.

Assault and battery: The combination of two violent crimes—assault (the threat of violence) and battery (crime) (physical violence).

Assault: Intentionally putting someone in reasonable apprehension of an imminent harmful or offensive contact; physical injury is not required.

Assessment center: An employee selection technique that allows human resource managers to observe and evaluate a prospective employee's performance on simulated tasks such as decision making and time management.

Assets: Items of value owned by the company.

Attitudes: Predispositions to respond favorably or unfavorably to something.

Attorney/client privilege: Communication made in confidence between a client and counsel for the purpose of seeking or providing legal counsel or advice.

At-will: An employee can be fired for any reason or for no reason at all.

Avoidance: Actions a person takes to escape from difficult thoughts and feelings.

Backbiting: Malicious talk about someone who is not present.

Backpay: Money that an employer owes an employee for work that he or she did in the past.

Backstabbing: *Verbal attack against someone who is not present, especially by a so-called friend.*

Basis: A basis is the "reason" being alleged for discrimination.

Battery: The actual act that causes physical harm.

Benchmarking: Comparing performance on specific dimensions with the performance of high-performing organizations.

Benefits (fringe): Indirect compensation paid to employees, such as health care, life insurance, vacations, and sick leave.

BFOQ: Bona fide occupational qualification.

Bias: A tendency to believe that some people, ideas, and so on, are better than others, which usually results in treating some people unfairly.

Bigotry: obstinate or intolerant devotion to one's own opinions and prejudices.

BLS: Bureau of Labor Statistics.

Botheration: The act or state of bothering or the state of being bothered.

Bothering: Annoying or pestering someone.

Bottom-up change: Change that is implemented gradually and involves managers and employees at all levels of an organization.

Browbeating: Intimidating by overbearing looks or words.

Burnout: A state of emotional, physical, and mental exhaustion caused by excessive and prolonged stress.

Bystander: A person who witnesses bias or B≈H.

Capital: Anything that confers value or benefit to its owners, such as its equipment or machinery, intellectual property such as patents, financial assets, or its employees.

Career counseling: Advice and assistance provided informally or formally to the individual regarding his career development and planning.

Career development: A careful, systematic approach to ensure that sound career choices that are made involves career planning (an individual element) and career management (an organizational element).

Career information systems: The combination of internal job markets with formal career counseling and the maintenance of a career information center for employees.

Career management: The organizational element of career development involving career counseling, career pathing, career resources planning, and career information systems.

Career pathing: Identifying coherent progressions of jobs (tracks, routes, or paths) that are of particular interest to the organization.

Career planning: Making detailed and specific decisions and plans about career goals and how to achieve them.

Career plateau: A position from which the chances of being promoted or obtaining a more responsible job are slight.

Career stages: Spans of years during which an individual has different types of concerns about job and career, sometimes labeled as the stages of career exploration, establishment, maintenance, and decline.

Career: A sequence of attitudes and behaviors that a person perceives to be related to work experience during his or her life. The sum total of work-related experiences throughout a person's life.

CDC: Centers for disease control.

CEA: Council of economic advisers.

Civil lawsuit: A court-based process through which Person A can seek to hold Person B liable for some type of harm or wrongful act.

Climate: The social environment of the organization.

Codes of conduct: Meaningful symbolic statements about the importance of adhering to high ethical standards in organizations.

Coercion: Using power or force to impose an unwanted behavior.

Cohesiveness: The extent to which group members are motivated to remain together.

Coming out: Disclosing a lesbian, gay, bisexual, or transgender/gender-expansive identity within themselves first and then choosing to reveal it to others.

Compensation: Wages and salaries paid to employees for their services.

Competitive advantage: The ability of one organization to outperform other organizations because it produces desired goods or services more efficiently and effectively than they do. The strategy component specifies the advantages the organization holds relative to its competitors.

Complainant: A person, group, or company that makes a complaint, as in a legal action (see also plaintiff).

Complaint: A complaint is an allegation of illegal discrimination.

Compliance: Going along with the boss's request but without any stake in the result.

Compromise: An agreement or a settlement of a dispute that is reached by each side making concessions.

Conflict of interest: A situation where the employee's decision may be compromised because of competing loyalties.

Conflict: Active disagreement between people with opposing opinions or principles.

Constructive discharge: Conditions are so hostile that the target is forced to leave work.

Consultants: Consultants are all consultants, vendors, or contractors engaged with over a predetermined period of time, and their safety and security might be in jeopardy.

Corroborate: Person or information that confirms or gives support to a statement, theory, or finding.

Credibility: Reputation as to believability.

Crisis management team: A group assembled at the top of an organization to develop plans and actions to prevent workplace violence.

Cyberbullying: Willful and repeated harm inflicted through the use of computers, cell phones, or other electronic devices.

Damages: A remedy in the form of a monetary award to be paid to a claimant as compensation for loss or injury.

Defaming: Making a false statement that injures someone's reputation or standing within a group.

Defendant: A person, company, and so on, against whom a claim or charge is brought in a court; person or entity being sued (see plaintiff).

Defense: The act of defending from or resisting attack.

Denigration: Sending or posting gossip or rumors about a person that damages that person's reputation or friendships.

Discipline: Punishment inflicted by way of correction and training.

Discovery: Obtaining and disclosing evidence and the position of each side of a case so that all parties involved can decide whether to move to trial or negotiate an early settlement.

Discrimination: Unfair treatment of one person or group of people because of the person or group's identity (e.g., race, gender, ability, religion, culture, etc.).

Disparaging terms: Words used to degrade individual characteristics.

Disparate impact: One group receives less favorable results than another.

Disparate treatment: One group is subjected to inconsistent application of rules and policies relative to others.

Disruptive: Behavior that causes difficulties interrupting performance or preventing it from continuing.

Diversity: Differences among people in age, gender, race, ethnicity, religion, sexual orientation, socioeconomic background, and capabilities/disabilities.

DOL: Department of Labor.

Downsizing: A reduction in organizational size and operating costs implemented by management to improve organizational efficiency, productivity, and/or the organization's competitiveness.

Dual-career families: Households in which both the husband and the wife are pursuing careers, not merely earning an income.

Dual-income families: Households in which both the husband and the wife earn a paycheck.

Due diligence: Reasonable steps taken by a person to satisfy parties and avoid harm to those involved.

Duress: Threats, violence, constraints, or other action brought to bear on an individual to do something against their will or better judgment.

Dysfunctional organization: An organization that undermines the purpose, health, wholeness, safety, solidarity, and worth of an organization or its stakeholders.

EBSA: Employee Benefits Security Administration.

ECAB: Employees' Compensation Appeals Board.

EEOC: The U.S. Equal Employment Opportunity Commission is responsible for enforcing federal laws that make it illegal to discriminate.

Effectiveness: Doing the right things in the right way at the right times. A measure of the appropriateness of the goals an organization is pursuing and of the degree to which the organization achieves those goals.

Empathy: The ability to identify and share feelings with someone.

Empire-building: Attempting to enlarge the size, scope, and influence of an individual or organization's power.

Employment at will: Freedom of the organization to employ someone when it desires and therefore to dismiss the employee at any time for any reason.

Empowerment: Expanding employees' tasks and responsibilities.

Enabling factors: Those things that improve your ability to manage unacceptable behavior that could lead to violence.

Enticement: Attracting by arousing hope or desire.

EPA: Equal Pay Act.

Equal Employment Opportunity Commission (EEOC): The agency responsible for enforcing federal laws regarding discrimination or harassment against job applicants or employees in the United States.

Equality: Having the same or similar rights and opportunities as others.

Equity: The quality of being fair or just.

Eroding factors: Those things that impede your ability to reduce unacceptable behavior that could lead to violence.

ESA: Employment Standards Administration; Economics and Statistics Administration.

ETA: Employment and Training Administration.

Ethical dilemma: A situation where the manager is faced with two or more conflicting ethical issues.

Ethics: A moral philosophy or code of morals practiced by a person or group of people.

Ethnic group: People who share a common religion, color, or national origin.

Evade: To endeavor to set aside truth or to escape punishment.

Evidence: The means by which any alleged matter is established or disproved.

Exclusion: Intentionally excluding someone from a group or its activities.

Fair labor practices: Equitable practices concerning hiring, wages, union relations, and so on.

FDA: Food and Drug Administration.

Feedback: Response from the receiver of a message to the sender of that message; for instance, telling the employee the results of his or her performance appraisal.

Filtering: Withholding part of a message out of the belief that the receiver does not need, will not want the information, or to intentionally deprive the receiver of important information.

Financial redress: Compensation for injuries sustained; recovery or restitution for harm or injury; damages or equitable relief.

FLRA: Federal Labor Relations Authority.

FMCS: Federal Mediation and Conciliation Service.

FMLA: Family and Medical Leave Act.

Front pay: Money awarded for lost compensation during the period between judgment and reinstatement, or if reinstatement is not feasible, instead of reinstatement.

Gender identity: One's deeply held core sense of being a girl/woman, boy/man, some of both, or neither.

Glass ceiling: A metaphor alluding to the invisible barriers that prevent minorities and women from being promoted to top corporate positions.

Gossiping: Spreading information that is usually incorrect about a person.

Grievance: A written statement or complaint filed by an employee with the union concerning the employee's alleged mistreatment by the company.

Group cohesiveness: The degree to which members are attracted or loyal to a group.

Group decision making: Choosing among alternatives by teams, committees, or other types of groups rather than by one individual.

Group norms: Shared guidelines or rules for behavior that most group members follow.

Group: Two or more people who interact regularly to accomplish a common goal; also see team.

Groupthink: A phenomenon that happens when the maintenance of cohesion and good feelings overwhelms the group's purpose. A pattern of faulty and biased decision making that occurs in groups whose members strive for agreement among themselves at the expense of accurately assessing information relevant to a decision.

Grudge: A feeling of ill will or resentment.

Harassment: A simple definition would be repeatedly sending offensive, rude, and insulting messages.

Harm: Physical or psychological damage or injury.

Hazing: Imposing humiliating or painful tasks.

HIPAA: Health Insurance Portability and Accountability Act.

HIV: Human immunodeficiency virus.

Hostile intruder (active shooter): An unrestrained individual within a contained area exercising the use of lethal force and posing an immediate risk of death or serious injury to area occupants, regardless of the type of lethal weapon involved.

Hostile work environment: The workplace creates a difficult or uncomfortable environment for another person to work in due to discrimination.

HPV: Human papillomavirus.

Hubris: A*n extreme and unreasonable feeling of pride and confidence in yourself.*

Human resource management (HRM): Activities that managers engage in to attract and retain employees and ensure that they perform at a high level and contribute to accomplishing organizational goals.

Humiliation: To reduce an individual to a lower position in one's or others' eyes: to embarrass or make them ashamed.

ICE: Immigration and Customs Enforcement.

Ignore: Refuse to take notice of or acknowledge; disregard intentionally.

ILAB: Bureau of International Labor Affairs.

ILO: International Labor Organization.

Inconsistency: A communication problem that exists when a person sends conflicting messages.

Inequality: An unfair situation when some individuals have more rights or better opportunities than others.

Inequity: Lack of fairness.

Informal organization: The overall pattern of influence and interaction defined by all the informal groups within an organization. The system of behavioral rules and norms that emerge in a group.

Initiative: The ability to act independently without a superior's direction.

Injunction: A court order requiring a person to do or cease doing a specific action.

Injustice: A situation in which the rights of a person or a group of people are ignored, disrespected, or discriminated against.

Innuendo: An indirect derogatory statement.

Intention: Something that you want and plan to do.

Internal terrorism: Behavior that involves the intent to evoke fear or extreme stress for the purpose of bringing about a change that benefits the perpetrator.

Interpersonal communication: Communication between people, especially small numbers of people, either orally, in writing, or nonverbally.

Intimidation: To force into or deter from some action by inducing fear.

Involvement: Taking part in something.

Jealousy: Feeling or showing envy of someone or their achievements and advantages.

LGBTQ: An acronym that collectively refers to individuals who are lesbian, gay, bisexual, transgender, or queer. It is sometimes stated as LGBT (lesbian, gay, bisexual, and transgender), GLBT (gay, lesbian, bi, and transgender).

Life stress: Events or experiences that produce severe strain, for example, bullying or harassment on the job.

Litigation: The process of resolving disputes by filing or answering a complaint through the court system.

Longevity: Suggests how long any given effort to deal with B≈H might be sustained.

MBDA: Minority Business Development Agency.

Mediation: A process wherein the parties meet with a mutually selected impartial and neutral person who assists them in negotiating their differences.

Menace: A person whose actions, attitudes, or ideas are considered dangerous or harmful.

Mental health: An individual's emotional, psychological, and social well-being that affects how they think, feel, and act.

Mentor: An experienced and trusted adviser.

Merit Systems Protection Board (MSPB): Federal agency responsible for dealing with personnel actions and appeals.

Mindset: An established set of attitudes held by someone.

Minority: A smaller group within a state, region, or country differs in race, religion, or national origin from the dominant group.

Molestation: Sexual assault or abuse of a person, especially a woman or a child.

Molesting: Assault or abuse (a person, especially a woman) sexually.

Murder: The premeditated killing of a person by another person.

Name-calling: The use of words to hurt, belittle, or be mean to someone or a group.

Narcissism: Self-centeredness; *an extreme and unreasonable feeling of pride and confidence in yourself.*

Negotiation: A method of conflict resolution in which the parties in conflict consider various alternative ways to allocate resources to each other in order to come up with a solution acceptable to them all.

Negotiator: A manager's role when attempting to work out agreements and contracts that operate in the organization's best interests.

Networking: The exchange of information through a group or network of interlinked computers.

NIH: National Institutes of Health.

NIOSH: The National Institute for Occupational Safety and Health is part of the CDC and is charged with developing new knowledge in the field of occupational safety and health and transferring that knowledge into practice.

NLRB: National Labor Relations Board.

NMB: National Mediation Board.

Nonverbal communication: Gestures and facial expressions that do not involve speaking but include nonverbal aspects of speech (tone and volume of voice, etc.).

Norm: A standard of behavior that the group develops for its members.

Normality: The condition or state of being usual, typical, or expected (normal).

OBL: Office of Business Liaison.

Occupational crime: Offenses that are committed by someone during the course of his or her employment.

Occupational deviant behavior: Self-serving deviant acts that occur at the workplace.

Offense: A perceived insult to or disregard for an individual.

OLMS: Office of Labor Management Standards.

On notice: Has received a notification so that one cannot claim to be unaware of a situation.

Organizational culture: Values and behaviors that contribute to an organization's unique social and psychological environment.

Organizational environment: The set of forces and conditions that operate beyond an organization's boundaries but affect a manager's ability to acquire and utilize resources.

Organizational politics: Individuals engage in activities to increase their power and use power effectively to achieve their goals and overcome resistance or opposition.

OSBP: Office of Small Business Programs.

OSDBU: Office of Small and Disadvantaged Business Utilization.

OSHA: The Occupational Safety and Health Administration is charged with ensuring safe and healthful working conditions for workers by setting and enforcing standards and by providing training, outreach, education, and assistance.

Ostracism: Being excluded from a group.

Outplacement: Support service provided by some organizations to help former employees transition to new jobs.

Overt discrimination: Knowingly and willingly denying diverse individuals access to organizational opportunities and outcomes.

OWBO: Office of Women's Business Ownership.

OWCP: Office of Workers' Compensation Programs.

Pain and suffering: The physical or emotional distress resulting from an injury.

Paranoia: Unjustified suspicion or distrust.

Participative management: Giving employees a voice in how things are done in organizations.

Perception: The recognition and interpretation of sensory information.

Perpetrator: A person who engages in unacceptable behavior or who carries out a harmful, illegal, or immoral act.

Persecution: Persistent annoyance, hostility, or ill-treatment, especially because of race or political or religious beliefs.

Personal injury: Physical injury inflicted on a person, as opposed to damage to property or reputation.

Pestering: Troubling or annoying an individual with frequent or persistent requests or interruptions.

Physical assault(s): Actually, hurting someone; also legally—intention, coupled with a present ability, of actual *violence* against a person, as by pointing a weapon at him when he is within reach of it (legal-dictionary.thefreedictionary.com). Shoving, pushing, hitting, kicking, fighting, and armed robbery.

Plaintiff: A person or entity filing a lawsuit (see defendant).

Positive approaches: Methods that stress prevention and support rather than punishment.

Power imbalance: A situation where one person or group has an advantage over others.

Power: An individual's ability to control or direct others.

Prank(s): Mischievous act(s) intended to harm or embarrass someone.

Predispositions: The tendency to perceive or act in a certain way because of previous experiences in one's background or environment.

Prejudice: Judging or having an idea about someone or a group of people before you actually know them.

Prima facie: This Latin for "on first view" or "at first appearance." In EEO cases, complainants present evidence and arguments to support a claim of discrimination.

Professional ethics: Standards that govern how members of a profession are to make decisions when the way they should behave is not clear-cut.

Property damage: Injury to real or personal property through another's negligence, willful destruction, or by some act of nature. In lawsuits for damages caused by negligence or a willful act, property damage is distinguished from personal injury (dictionary.law.com).

Protect(ing): Keeping safe from mental or physical harm or injury.

Protected class: Groups protected from employment discrimination by law.

Protection: The action of protecting, or the state of being protected.

Psychological harm: Something that results in mental or emotional trauma or that leads to behavioral change or physical symptoms that require psychological or psychiatric care.

Psychological trauma: An emotional response to a terrible event such as an accident, rape, or natural disaster. Immediately after the event, shock and denial are typical (www.apa.com).

Psychosocial hazard or risk: Aspects of the social design or management that have the potential for causing psychological or physical harm.

Public apology: Apologizing in the presence of others.

Punishment: Administering an undesired or negative consequence when dysfunctional behavior occurs; reprimands, discipline, fines, and so on, which are used to shape behavior by causing a reduction in unwanted behaviors.

Punitive damages: Damages assessed in the legal process to punish a defendant and to prevent him or her from hurting others by the same or similar actions.

Pushing: Shoving someone, usually with a hand.

Quid pro quo: A manager or other authority figure offers or merely hints that he or she will give the employee something (a raise or a promotion) in return for that employee's satisfaction of a sexual demand.

Racism: Prejudice and/or discrimination against people because of their racial group.

Rareness: The capability of managing the contributing factors to B≈H within the organization.

Reasonable person standard: A test in personal injury cases that jurors use to determine if a defendant acted like other people would have in the same situation.

Recruiting: The process of attracting a pool of qualified applicants who are interested in working for the company.

Redress: The setting right of what is wrong.

Remedies: A form of court enforcement of a legal right resulting from a successful civil lawsuit.

Resistance: The negative, uncooperative response of people when their boss attempts to influence them.

Retaliation: An employer punishes an employee for engaging in legally protected activity.

Rumors: Unofficial pieces of information of interest to organizational members but with no identifiable source.

Sabotage: Acting to deliberately destroy, damage, or obstruct (something), especially in retaliation.

Safe harbor rooms (safe rooms): A predetermined interior, windowless area/room, or any room of the office/facility that can provide a temporary barrier in protecting occupants from external dangers posed by a hostile intruder(s).

Safeguard: A measure taken to protect someone or something or to prevent something undesirable.

Safety audit: A systematic process that evaluates a workplace's health and safety.

Safety: The condition of being protected from or unlikely to cause danger, risk, or injury.

SBA: Small Business Administration.

Security: Being free from danger or threat.

Self-efficacy: Your belief in your own abilities to deal with various situations.

Sexting: Sending sexually explicit photographs or messages via mobile phone or other electronic means.

Sexual harassment: Unwelcome sexual advances, requests for sexual favors, or other verbal or physical conduct of a sexual nature.

Shelter-in-place (immediate protective measures): A defensive action that employees and others can take to protect themselves against a hazard such as an armed hostile intruder, and in circumstances in which there has been an insufficient warning to escape and evacuate the offices, facilities, buildings, work areas, or safely enter the Safe Harbor Room.

Shunning: An act of social rejection or emotional distancing.

Smoothing: Downplaying the importance of a problem.

Stalking: Following someone stealthily to cause them fear.

Stereotype: False idea that all group members are the same and/or think and behave in the same way.

Stress: A feeling of emotional strain and pressure.

Strict liability: Imposes legal responsibility for damages or injuries even if the person who was found strictly liable did not act with fault or negligence.

Swearing: Using offensive language.

Tagout: Disabling machinery so it cannot be used.

Target: Someone who is subject to unacceptable behavior or treated in hurtful ways by a person or a group on purpose and over and over.

Team-building: A series of activities and exercises designed to enhance the motivation and satisfaction of people in groups by fostering mutual understanding, acceptance, and group cohesion.

Team: A group whose members work intensely with each other to achieve a specific, common goal or objective.

Teasing: Persistently annoying someone, especially with jokes that may even be about them.

Terror: Violence or threats of violence used for intimidation or coercion.

Terrorism: Intimidation or coercion by instilling fear.

Theft: Stealing; robbing.

Third-party harassment: Harassment by someone who is not a member of the organization (e.g., customer, supplier).

Threat: The implication or expression of intent to inflict physical harm or actions that a reasonable person would interpret as a threat to physical safety or property.

Title VII: Part of the Civil Rights Act of 1964 is a federal law that protects employees against discrimination based on certain specified characteristics: race, color, national origin, sex, and religion.

Tolerance: The willingness to accept opinions, behaviors, and characteristics different from one's own.

Traits: Characteristics of a person.

Transgender: Term for people whose gender identity differs from that assigned at birth (e.g., assigned female or male).

Trust: A belief in the reliability, truth, ability, or strength of someone or something.

Turnover: The number or percentage of workers who leave an organization and are replaced by new employees.

Unwelcome conduct: Any behavior by subordinates, peers, or superiors that is deemed offensive or unwelcome by an employee.

Value: The organization's productivity and its value to customers, clients, and employees.

Vandalism: Deliberate destruction of or damage to property.

Vengeance: Infliction of injury, harm, humiliation, or the like, on a person by another whom that person has harmed.

Verbal abuse: Making profane or antagonizing remarks in an attempt to annoy, anger, or harass.

V-REEL: Framework, originally developed for strategic analysis in organizations (Flint, 2018), provides a unique way of thinking about the causes of unacceptable behavior that might lead to violence and how to eradicate it. It consists of five components—Value, Rareness, Eroding factors, Enabling factors, and Longevity.

Vulnerable individuals: Those who are or may be, for any reason, unable to take care of themselves, or unable to protect themselves against significant harm or exploitation.

Well-being: Coping with day-to-day stress, working productively, and interacting positively with others.

Whistle-blower: A person who reports illegal or unethical behavior.

Withdrawal: Avoiding people and activities you would usually enjoy; social isolation.

Workplace violence: Behavior in which an employee, former employee, visitor, or service provider to a workplace inflicts or threatens serious harm, injury, or death to others at the workplace or inflicts damage to property. This behavior is pertinent in workplaces as defined as an official workplace or company-sponsored event.

Zero-tolerance: A standard that establishes that any implied or actual behavior that violates the policy will not be tolerated.

Notes

Chapter 1

1. Sutton, *Good Bosses Bad Bosses*, 59.

Chapter 5

1. Leaderchat, "A Mini Case Study On Motivation."

Chapter 6

1. Nater, Van Fleet, and Van Fleet, *Combating Workplace Violence: Creating and Maintaining Safe Work Environments*.
2. Healthcare Industries, "Carolinas HealthCare System In Case Studies in Occupational Health and Safety Management."

Chapter 7

1. Clark, *The 4 Stages of Psychological Safety*.
2. Helbig, and Norman, *Psychological Safety Playbook*.
3. Niruta Publications, "Nurturing Psychological Safety In the Workplace."

Chapter 8

1. Van Fleet, *Dysfunctional Organizations: How to Remove Obstacles to Psychological Safety*.
2. V-Reel-For-The-Whole-Family.

Chapter 9

1. Gallo, A. "What Is Psychological Safety?"
2. Rigby, "Real-Life Examples Proving Psychological Safety Is Crucial."
3. Insights, "What Is Psychological Safety in the Workplace? How Leaders Can Build Psychologically Safe Workplaces."

Chapter 10

1. Hagen, "The Humanist Ten Commandments."

Glossary

1. Van Fleet, *Dysfunctional Organizations: How to Remove Obstacles to Psychological Safety.*

References and Recommended Readings

1. Van Fleet, *Dysfunctional Organizations: How to Remove Obstacles to Psychological Safety.*

References and Recommended Readings[1]

Allas, T., and B. Weddle. 2022. "Meet the Psychological Needs of Your People—All Your People." *McKinsey Quarterly.*

American Psychological Association. 2024. "What Is Psychological Safety at Work? Here's How to Start Creating It." *American Psychological Association.* March 4. www.apa.org/topics/healthy-workplaces/psychological-safety.

AmTrust Financial. 2019. "ROI of Safety: How to Create a Long-Term Profitable Workplace Safety Program." *AmTrust Financial.* https://amtrustfinancial.com/getmedia/d6d1ecf6-1ad1-4e19-84ae-f0fd1991f761/ROI-Safety-Final-Report.pdf.

Anonymous. 2020. "How Important Is Psychological Safety, Really?" *Kudos.* www.kudos.com/blog/how-important-is-psychological-safety-really.

Attfield, B. 2019. "7 Ways to Create Psychological Safety at Work." *Jostle Blog.* https://blog.jostle.me/blog/psychological-safety-at-work.

Barnett, G. n.d. "8 Ways to Create Psychological Safety in the Workplace." *The Predictive Index.* www.predictiveindex.com/blog/psychological-safety-in-the-workplace/.

Battye, G. n.d. "The 5 Pillars of Psychological Safety." *Gina Battye.* www.ginabattye.com/5-pillars-psychological-safety/.

Bosler, S. 2021. "9 Strategies to Create Psychological Safety at Work." *Quantum Workplace.* www.quantumworkplace.com/future-of-work/create-psychological-safety-in-the-workplace.

Bronkhorst, B. 2015. "Behaving Safely under Pressure: The Effects of Job Demands, Resources, and Safety Climate on Employee Physical and Psychosocial Safety Behavior." *Journal of Safety Research* 55: 63-72.

Cable, D. 2018. "How Humble Leadership Really Works." *Harvard Business Review.* https://hbr.org/2018/04/how-humble-leadership-really-works.

Carbajal, E. 2024. "Psychological Safety at Work Has Downsides, Studies Show." *Becker's Hospital Review.* www.beckershospitalreview.com/workforce/psychological-safety-at-work-has-downsides-studies-show.html.

Casabianca, S.S. 2022. "How to Create Psychological Safety at Work and Why It Makes a Difference." *PsychCentral.* https://psychcentral.com/health/psychological-safety-at-work.

Center for Creative Leadership. 2023. "What Is Psychological Safety at Work? How Leaders Can Build Psychologically Safe Workplaces." *Center for Creative Leadership.* Available at: www.ccl.org/articles/leading-effectively-articles/

what-is-psychological-safety-at-work/#:~:text=Psychological%20safety%20
is%20the%20belief,taking%20risks%2C%20or%20soliciting%20feedback.

Clark, T.R. 2022. "What Psychological Safety Is Not." *Forbes*.www.forbes.com/
sites/timothyclark/2021/06/21/what-psychological-safety-is-not/.

Clark, T.R. 2020. *The 4 Stages of Psychological Safety*. Oakland, CA: Berrett-
Koehler Publishers, Inc.

Cooper, L. 2023. "The Relationship Between Performance and Psychological
Safety." *Training Industry*.https://trainingindustry.com/articles/performance-
management/the-relationship-between-performance-and-psychological-
safety/.

Dollard, M. F., and A.B. Bakker. 2010. "Psychosocial Safety Climate as a
Precursor to Conducive Work Environments, Psychological Health Problems,
and Employee Engagement." *Journal of Occupational and Organizational
Psychology* 83: 579–599.

Deming, W.E. 2018. *The New Economics for Industry, Government, Education*, 3rd
ed. Cambridge, MA: MIT Press.

DuBrin, A.J. 2009. *Essentials of Management*, 8th ed. Mason, OH: Thomson
Business & Economics.

Dweck, C.S. 2016. *Mindset: The Psychology of Success*. New York: Penguin
Random House LLC.

Edmondson, A.C. 1996. "Learning from Mistakes Is Easier Said Than Done:
Group and Organizational Influences on the Detection and Correction of
Human Error." *The Journal of Applied Behavioral Science* 32 (1): 5–28.

Edmondson, A.C. 2004. "Psychological Safety, Trust, and Learning in
Organizations: A Group-Level Lens." In *Trust and Distrust in Organizations:
Dilemmas and Approaches*, edited by R.M. Kramer and K.S. Cook, 239–72.
New York,NY: Russell Sage.

Edmondson, A.C. 2012. *Teaming: How Organizations Learn, Innovate, and
Compete in the Knowledge Economy*. New York,NY: John Wiley & Sons. ISBN
978-0-7879-70932.

Edmondson, A.C. 2013. *Teaming to Innovate*. New York,NY: John Wiley &
Sons. ISBN 978-1118856277.

Edmondson, A.C. 2018. *The Fearless Organization: Creating Psychological Safety
in the Workplace for Learning, Innovation, and Growth*. New York,NY: John
Wiley & Sons. ISBN 978-1119477242.

Edmondson, A.C. 2023. *Right Kind of Wrong: The Science of Failing Well*. New
York,NY: Atria Books.

Edmondson, A. C., and D.P. Bransby. 2023. "Psychological Safety Comes of
Age: Observed Themes in an Established Literature." *Annual Review of
Organizational Psychology and Organizational Behavior* 10 (1): 55–78.

Edmondson, A. C., J.R. Dillon, and K.S. Roloff. 2007. "Three Perspectives on Team Learning: Outcome Improvement, Task Mastery, and Group Process." *Academy of Management Annals* 1: 269–314.

Edmondson, A.C., and S.S. Reynolds. 2016. *Building the Future: Big Teaming for Audacious Innovation.* United States: Berrett-Koehler Publishers, Inc.

Edmondson, A.C., and J.F. Harvey. 2017. *Extreme Teaming: Lessons in Complex, Cross-Sector Leadership.* London, United Kingdom,UK: Emerald Publishing Limited.

Edmondson, A.C., and J.F. Harvey. 2018. "Cross-Boundary Teaming for Innovation: Integrating Research on Teams and Knowledge in Organizations." *Human Resource Management Review* 28 (4): 347–360.

Edmondson, A. C., and P. Hugander. 2021. "4 Steps to Boost Psychological Safety at Your Workplace." *Harvard Business Review.*https://hbr.org/2021/06/4-steps-to-boost-psychological-safety-at-your-workplace.

Edmondson, A. C., and Z. Lei. 2014. "Psychological Safety: The History, Renaissance, and Future of an Interpersonal Construct." *Annual Review of Organizational Psychology and Organizational Behavior* 1: 23–43.

Eldor, L., M. Hodor, and P. Cappelli. 2023. "The Limits of Psychological Safety: Nonlinear Relationships with Performance." *Organizational Behavior and Human Decision Processes* 177 (C).

Eldor, L., and P. Cappelli. 2024. "Can Workplaces Have Too Much Psychological Safety?" *Harvard Business Review.*https://hbr.org/2024/01/can-workplaces-have-too-much-psychological-safety.

Ferrère, A., C. Rider, B. Renerte, and A.C. Edmondson. 2022. "Fostering Ethical Conduct through Psychological Safety." *MIT Sloan Management Review* 63 (4): 39–43.

Flint, D. 2018. *Think Beyond Value: Building Strategy to Win.* New York, NY: Morgan James Publishing.

Gallo, A. 2023. "What Is Psychological Safety?" *Harvard Business Review.* https://hbr.org/2023/02/what-is-psychological-safety.

Gomez-Mejia, L. R., D.B. Balkin, and R.L. Cardy. 2008. *Management: People, Performance, Change,* 3rd ed. New York: McGraw-Hill.

Griffin, R.W. 2022. *Fundamentals of Management,* 10th ed. Boston, MA: Cengage.

Hagen, C. 2013. "The Humanist Ten Commandments." The Humanist.com, October 30. https://thehumanist.com/commentary/the-humanist-ten-commandments/.

Helbig, K., and M. Norman. 2023. *Psychological Safety Playbook.* Las Vegas, NV: Pagetwo.

Healthcare Industries. 2013. "Carolinas HealthCare System in Case Studies in Occupational Health and Safety Management." https://code-authorities. ul.com/wp-content/uploads/sites/40/2015/02/Case_Studies_in_ Occupational_Health_and_Safety_Management.pdf.

Howatt, B. 2024. "The Dark Side of the Psychological Health and Safety Conversation." *OHS Canada*.www.ohscanada.com/features/the-dark-side-of-the-psychological-health-and-safety-conversation/.

Idris, M.A., M.F. Dollard, and M.R. Tuckey. 2015. "Psychosocial Safety Climate as a Management Tool for Employee Engagement and Performance: A Multilevel Analysis." *International Journal of Stress Management* 22 (2): 183–206. https://doi.org/10.1037/a0038986.

Insights. 2023. "What Is Psychological Safety in the Workplace? How Leaders can Build Psychologically Safe Workplaces. www.greatplacetowork.com/resources/blog/psychological-safety-workplace.

Jansen, L. 2021. "The Danger of Psychological Safety." *LinkedIn*. www.linkedin.com/pulse/danger-psychological-safety-laura-jansen-she-her-/.

Jay, S. n.d. "What Is a Psychological Contract: Types with Examples." *Academy to Innovate HR*.www.aihr.com/blog/psychological-contract/.

Jiang, Z., X. Hu, Z. Wang, and X. Jiang. 2019. "Knowledge Hiding as a Barrier to Thriving: The Mediating Role of Psychological Safety and Moderating Role of Organizational Cynicism." *Journal of Organizational Behavior* 40: 800–818.

Jiménez, J. 2022. "Why Psychological Safety at Work Matters and How to Create It." *BetterUp*.www.betterup.com/blog/why-psychological-safety-at-work-matters.

Kahn, W.A. 1990. "Psychological Conditions of Personal Engagement and Disengagement at Work." *Academy of Management Journal* 33 (4): 692–724.

Kaloudis, H. 2019. "Is Your Team at Work Psychologically Safe?" *Bluefire Leadership*.https://bluefireleadership.com/psychologically-safe/.

Kotter, J.P. 1996. *Leading Change*. Boston, MA: Harvard Business Review Press.

Leaderchat. 2013. "A Mini Case Study on Motivation ." https://leaderchat.org/2013/03/04/a-mini-case-study-on-motivation/.

Lennox, E. 2021. "Do We Need Psychological Safety or Psychosocial Safety? What's the Difference?" *LinkedIn*.www.linkedin.com/pulse/do-we-need-psychological-safety-psychosocial-whats-elena-lennox/?trk=pulse-article_more-articles_related-content-card.

Loignon, A., and S. Wormington. 2022. "Psychologically Safe for Some, but Not All?" *Center for Creative Leadership*. Available at: https://cclinnovation.org/wp-content/uploads/2022/05/psychologicallysafe.pdf?webSyncID=4a6283cb-bae2-894a-c5dd-4d9cd70c102e&sessionGUID=834e2ea5-7576-2d62-95b3-b7102ee168aa. DOI: https://doi.org/10.35613/ccl.2022.204.

MacArthur, H.V. 2023. "Psychological Safety: Minimizing the Silent Enemies of a Thriving Team." *Forbes*.www.forbes.com/sites/hvmacarthur.

Maheshwari, S.K. 2007. *Turnaround Excellence: Six Studies of Corporate Renewal*. New York, NY: Penguin Random House LLC.

Mansour, S., M. Faisal Azeem, M. Dollard, and R. Potter. 2022. "How Psychosocial Safety Climate Helped Alleviate Work Intensification Effects on Presenteeism during the COVID-19 Crisis? A Moderated Mediation Model." *International Journal of Environmental Research and Public Health* 19 (20): 13673.10.3390/ijerph192013673. PMID: 36294252; PMCID: PMC9603230.

Maximo, N., M.W. Stander, and L. Coxen. 2019. "Authentic Leadership and Work Engagement: The Indirect Effects of Psychological Safety and Trust in Supervisors." *SA Journal of Industrial Psychology* 45 (1): 1–11.

Michael, D.N. 1976. *On Learning to Plan and Planning to Learn*. San Francisco, CA: Jossey-Bass.

Mlynek, J. 2021. "Investing in Safety - Every Dollar Spent Saves Company $3 to $5." *Grainnet Safety*. www.grainnetsafety.com/article/232910/investing-in-safety-every-dollar-spent-saves-a-company-3-to-5.

Nater, F., D.D. Van Fleet, and E.W. Van Fleet. 2023. *Combating Workplace Violence: Creating and Maintaining Safe Work Environments*. Charlotte, NC: Information Age Publishing.

National Association of Safety Professionals (NASP). 2023. "Guide to Psychosocial Safety." https://naspweb.com/blog/guide-to-psychosocial-safety/.

National Safety Council. n.d. "Case Study Implementing Psychological Safety Interventions at a Corporate Lending Firm." safer-case-study-psychological-safety-corp-lending-firm.pdf.

Newman, A., R. Donohue, and N. Eva. 2017. "Psychological Safety: A Systematic Review of the Literature." *Human Resource Management Review* 27 (3): 521–535.

Niruta Publications. 2023. "Nurturing Psychological Safety in the Workplace: The Rishika Case Study ." www.nirutapublications.org/hr-blog/nurturing-psychological-safety-in-the-workplace-the-rishika-case-study.

O'Donohoe, J., and K. Kleinschmit. 2022. "Setting the Stage for Psychological Safety: 6 Steps for Leaders." *Health University of Utah*. https://accelerate.uofuhealth.utah.edu/resilience/setting-the-stage-for-psychological-safety-6-steps-for-leaders.

Praslova, L. N., R. Carucci, and C. Stokes. 2022. "How Bullying Manifests at Work — and How to Stop It." *Harvard Business Review*. https://hbr.org/2022/11/how-bullying-manifests-at-work-and-how-to-stop-it.

Qualls, M., and the CultureAlly Team. 2022. "What Is Psychological Safety?" *CultureAlly*. https://www.cultureally.com/blog/whatispsychologicalsafety.

Radecki, D., L. Hull, J. McCusker, and C. Ancona. 2018. *Psychological Safety: The Key to Happy, High-Performing People and Teams.* Orange County, CA: The Academy of Brain-Based Leadership.

Radecki, J., and C. Ancona. 2021. *Psychological Safety.* Orange County, CA: The Academy of Brain-Based Leadership.

Ravishankar, R.A. 2022. "A Guide to Building Psychological Safety on Your Team." *Harvard Business Review.* https://hbr.org/2022/12/a-guide-to-building-psychological-safety-on-your-team.

Rigby, A. 2024. "Real-Life Examples Proving Psychological Safety Is Crucial." https://getmarlee.com/blog/psychological-safety.

Robert I. Sutton. Good Bosses Bad Bosses, 59 New York, NY: Balance Hachette Book Group.

Ryba, K. 2021. "Making Time and Space for Performance Management." November 23. https://rb.gy/k7l4g.

Schein, E.H. 1993. "How Can Organizations Learn Faster? The Challenge of Entering the Green Room." *Sloan Management Review* 34: 85–92.

Schein, E. H., and W.G. Bennis. 1965. *Personal and Organizational Change Through Group Methods.* New York,NY: John Wiley & Sons.

Scorza, J. 2018. "Drive Innovation with Psychological Safety." *SHRM Book Blog.* www.linkedin.com/pulse/do-we-need-psychological-safety-psychosocial-whats-elena-lennox/?trk=pulse-article_more-articles_related-content-card.

Stefirta, A. n.d. "The Risks of Poor Collaboration in the Workplace." www.teamly.com/blog/lack-of-collaboration-in-the-workplace/.

Taylor, J., D. Collins, and M. Ashford. 2022. "Psychological Safety in High-Performance Sport: Contextually Applicable?" *Frontiers in Sports Active Living.* www.ncbi.nlm.nih.gov/pmc/articles/PMC9125081/.

Thiede, I., and M. Thiede. 2015. "Quantifying the Costs and Benefits of Occupational Health and Safety Interventions at a Bangladesh Shipbuilding Company." *International Journal of Occupational and Environmental Health* 21 (2): 127–136. 10.1179/2049396714Y.0000000100. PMID: 25589369; PMCID: PMC4457121.

Tiwari, B., and U. Lenka. 2016. "Building Psychological Safety for Employee Engagement in Post-Recession." *Development and Learning in Organizations* 30 (1): 19–22. https://doi.org/10.1108/DLO-05-2015-0044.

Van der Loo, H., and J. Beks. 2020. *Psychological Safety,* 2nd ed. Amsterdam: Boom. Independently published.

Van Fleet, D.D., and T.O. Peterson. 1994. *Contemporary Management,* 3rd ed. Boston: Houghton Mifflin.

Van Fleet, D.D. 2024. *Dysfunctional Organizations: How to Remove Obstacles to Psychological Safety.* New York,NY: Business Expert Press.

Van Fleet, E.W., and D.D. Van Fleet. 2007. *Workplace Survival: Dealing with Bad Bosses, Bad Workers, Bad Jobs*. Frederick, MD: PublishAmerica.

V-Reel-for-the-Whole-Family. 2020 . https://drdavidflint.com/2018/08/16/v-reel-for-the-whole-family/.

Weaver, B., A. Kirk-Brown, D. Goodwin, and J. Oxley. 2023. "Psychosocial Safety Behavior: A Scoping Review of Behavior-Based Approaches to Workplace Psychosocial Safety." *Journal of Safety Research* 84: 33–40.

Weinstein, M. 2023. "How Much Psychological Safety Is Too Much?" *Training Day Blog*. https://trainingmag.com/how-much-psychological-safety-is-too-much/.

Wegner, A. n.d. "5 Steps to Create Psychological Safety in the Workplace." www.babbelforbusiness.com/us/blog/psychological-safety-at-work/.

Yaris, C., G. Ditchburn, G.J. Curtis, and L. Brook. 2020. "Combining Physical and Psychosocial Safety: A Comprehensive Workplace Safety Model." *Safety Science* 132: 1–9.

About the Author

David D. Van Fleet is professor emeritus of Management in the Morrison School of Agribusiness, W.P. Carey School of Business at Arizona State University. He is a past editor of both the *Journal of Management* and the *Journal of Behavioral and Applied Management*. He is or has been a member of the Board of Governors, Academy of Management, Southwest Federation of Academic Disciplines, and the Southern Management Association, and was the national chair of the Management History Division of the Academy of Management. He is a fellow of both the Academy of Management and the Southern Management Association. He has been listed in Who's Who in the World, Who's Who in America, Who's Who Among America's Teachers, and Who's Who in Agriculture Academia. He has over 300 publications and presentations, including 15 books and several websites for students. He has over 50 years of full-time teaching experience, including 64 different courses.

Index

www.ingramcontent.com/pod-product-compliance
Lightning Source LLC
Chambersburg PA
CBHW061317220326
41599CB00026B/4917